YOUNG

and

D<u>RIVEN</u>

OVERDRIVE

BY

DR. CORTLAN J. WICKLIFF, ESQ.

Overdrive Edition: November 2019
First Edition: April 2017

ISBN: 978-0-9989698-2-4

For the men and women that presented me with consistently high benchmarks to achieve. Every day I strive towards the standards of excellence, integrity and compassion you set for me. Thank you for being the giants on whose shoulders I stand; I hope that I can push others towards success the same way you pushed me!

Table of Contents

Foreword

My eyes still well up as I recall the tragedy that drove my son to become Dr. Cortlan James Wickliff, Esq.

I sat in the living room waiting on my son Cortlan to come home from school asking myself, "How do you communicate extremely devastating news to a 10-year-old child?" Amid my numbness and excruciating pain, as the author of this book walked through the door after school that dreadful afternoon in October of 2000, that is exactly what I had to do. Unsuccessfully straining to hold back tears, I managed to utter the unthinkable. "Your dad died last night from a heart attack in his sleep…"

That was the longest-short conversation I had ever had. He didn't really ask many questions, break down crying, or react with the disbelief or confusion I had expected. Instead, he said, "I better go tell coach I won't be at practice for a bit," and he immediately walked out of the door. Did he understand what had just happened? Was he in shock? That was a dark day. However, what happens in the next few days is nothing short of amazing and I believe divinely orchestrated.

But first a little about Cortlan... Anybody who hears his story invariably wants to know, "when did you know he was different."

His dad and I discovered that we had a unique child, back at the beginning of the summer of 1994, when he was 3yrs old. That summer, like we did most summers, we brought several of our nieces and nephews to stay with us and participate in local summer programs. This particular year, I was a bit overzealous. I somehow piled 7 or more kids in my little Geo Metro and made the 4-hour-trip from Liberty, Texas to our home in Austin. Seeing the clown-car like scene of all those people getting out of a vehicle barely bigger than a Toyota Prius, made Tony (Cortlan's dad) decide we needed to have a family meeting. During this meeting, his dad discussed the schedule for household chores with his older two brothers and I.

As the meeting ended, Tony reiterated the assignment of chores and expectations of everyone in our home. The only person he did not directly address was 3-year-old Cortlan. Tony then ended the meeting, so he thought, with a pair of questions.

Tony: ***Do you all understand? Does anyone have anything to say?***

After an extended silence, the smallest person in the room boldly proclaimed in his full voice:

Cortlan: ***Yes, daddy. If no one else has anything to say, I have something to say.***

Surprised to receive any feedback, let alone feedback from his youngest son, Tony asked him what he wanted to say.

Cortlan replied, "The way I see it, Daddy, it sounds like you are ready to be the boss of the house now, and if you are ready to be the boss, you need to do things for yourself..."

We were stunned. His brothers were terrified, his dad was irritated, and his cousins in the next room got extremely quiet. If it had stopped there, it would have been enough. But Tony, being a mix of irritated and curious asked, "Is there anything else."

Cortlan gladly volunteered specifics oblivious to how irritated the man sitting next to him was becoming. Cortlan proceeded to tell his father that he should not request his children to get things like his ashtray or cigarettes, but get them himself. Despite Tony turning a brighter shade of red by the second, he kept asking Cortlan for more. Cortlan continued to freely share, "And the way I see it, the boss should pay the bills, too."

Angrily Tony inquired, "Since you know so much, what do you suggest that I pay?"

Boldly and naively Cortlan continued, "The way I see it, if mom pays the house bill, you can pay my school bill; and if mom pays the light bill, you can pay the 'sink' bill." The phrase "sink-bill" reminded everyone in the house that Cortlan was only 3 years old. At that moment, my nieces and nephews in the next room erupted in laughter, Cortlan's brothers let out some giggles, and even I chuckled a bit.

Nevertheless, Tony was not distracted by the laughter, and Cortlan didn't get the joke. Tony undeterred, stone-faced, and red with anger asked if there was anything else. Completely oblivious to the danger he was in, Cortlan, yet again said, "The way I see it..."

Before he could utter another word, I took the chaotic laughter as a nice break to stop the conversation and send all the kids outside to play.

Tony was convinced that I had put Cortlan up to saying all of those things, or that he was repeating something that I had said. I, of course, had nothing to do with Cortlan's expressed opinion. Back then people could only pay bills by mail or in person. There was no online option. Thus, whenever I had a bill to pay, I would pay them while taking Cortlan to and from school each day. Like most kids his age, Cortlan asked a lot of questions, and I answered them. I recall inquiries like:

He asked, "What are you doing Mommy?" I replied, "I am mailing the mortgage payment for our house."

He'd ask, "Why are you mailing those?" I responded, "When you are an adult you have to pay bills." –Or–

He would ask, "Mommy, what's that piece of paper?" and I'd reply, "It's a check to pay for your school." etc.

After Cortlan's exchange with Tony, I realized that while running errands and entertaining the curious questions of my toddler son, Cortlan had been observing and drawing conclusions of his own. This level of deductive reasoning was well beyond the scope of a typical child his age. Because of that fact, it was utterly impossible trying to convince my husband that I had nothing to do with it. This meant that Tony spent the entire summer thinking I was trying to "poison his son against him."

Though the rest of the summer was a bit awkward in our home, early in the fall semester I would be exonerated.

His dad soon found out for himself just how inquisitive and 'helpful' Cortlan could be. In the fall, Cortlan was 4 years old and starting Pre-Kindergarten school. Tony decided that, instead of paying for afterschool daycare, he would watch Cortlan at his auto-body and paint shop in the afternoons. This would have been a great way to save money if Tony had lasted more than a week.

A few days into the first week of school, I received a call from Tony. "Come get Cortlan as soon as possible!"

I frantically asked what was wrong. In that moment, my mind was flooded with the horrible images of our 4-year-old having hurt himself with one of my husband's industrial tools. Tony, oblivious to my fears, went on to

4

explain that Cortlan had taken it upon himself to organize the tool area in the shop, stating safety concerns; he had also prepared a phone script for the receptionist answering the phone to better give customer updates. Tony said that he was generally trying to run his business! His employees got a big laugh out of the whole situation because, per them, Cortlan was actually doing a good job. This put Tony on the receiving end of several jokes about his son running the business better than he did. Needless to say, Tony gladly paid for afterschool care from that point on.

Despite an occasional, unique, uncharacteristic event like the few mentioned above, Cortlan displayed otherwise very normal child-like behavior. He played soccer, liked his chemistry set, loved movies and enjoyed playing with his family and friends. However, he did seem to always be thinking and analyzing even when he wasn't sharing his thoughts. So, in October of 2000 when his dad died, I was very concerned about how this might affect him. On the day of his dad's funeral, I got my first glimpse of the impact Tony's untimely death would have on Cortlan.

We were midway through the funeral and had just concluded the portion of the program whereby several people had shared fond memories and expressed words of comfort to the family. I was in such pain; I just wanted it to be over. The preacher was at the lectern preparing to share the scripture for the eulogy when Cortlan stood up and walked to the microphone that was still located near his father's coffin. I guess Cortlan had thought about giving expressions but as a child attending his first funeral, he did not realize that we had proceeded passed that portion of the program. The preacher, however, was gracious and yielded the floor to Cortlan. Many of us were in shock and had no idea what to expect as Cortlan had never spoken in such a public event. What did a child have to say, especially on an occasion such as this? He cleared his throat and with his voice a bit shaky he began to speak.

"Hello everyone. My name is Cortlan Wickliff. I am 10 years old and I am the youngest child of Tony Wickliff. I was sitting there thinking about everything. I still can hardly believe that this is real. I wish it wasn't. I keep waiting on him to sit up in the casket and start laughing at all of us for having these sad faces. I really learned a lot from my dad, including how to be strong – mostly from him joking and picking with me." Since the audience knew Tony's character as a fun-loving jokester, that statement provoked the audience to release a loud laugh that seemed to relax Cortlan a bit. He continued. *"God is a good God and He would not have taken my dad unless my dad had done all that God wanted him to do here on Earth. Since my dad obviously completed his purpose for being here, God took him on to heaven. Now it is all of our responsibilities to do the same. We have to find out what is our God-given purpose and then make sure that we get busy doing it so we can fulfill our purpose too like my dad did, before God calls us home. Thank you."*

There was not a dry eye in the packed church as everyone rushed to their feet and gave a standing ovation that seemed to last for several minutes. Cortlan had spoken in church and recited prewritten speeches in school. I call this his first public speech because this was the first time he stood up and delivered his own words un-coached and unassisted. And for the majority of the family, it was their first time seeing what his father and I had learned 6 years earlier; there was something unique about him.

For Cortlan, I believe it was his public declaration of the start of a journey to live a purpose-driven life. Soon afterward, he shared with me the positive impact that he planned to have on society. He would start that journey by achieving those seemingly farfetched academic goals he had set years earlier. This time, though, there was something different about the way he said it.

He began to set short-term goals, get focused, develop plans, follow them and achieve each goal. Then he would set another goal, achieve it and repeat. He allowed the tragedy of his father's death to chart a trajectory for his journey that has already resulted in historic achievements.

This book contains a roadmap of how he did it. Honestly, it was sometimes challenging to be the type of supportive parent that Cortlan required. For instance, when

he was accepted to college at age 14, he had to move 250 miles away from home into the university dorm only a week after his 15th birthday. I learned how to encourage, pray and be a voice of reason for him, sometimes all in the same conversation. Above all, I was always his parent first, even from a distance. His journey required me to suppress my fears and worries often, to help him mature and grow through his challenges. More about that in the next book...

For now, as his mother and now a professional peer, his achievements in spite of very difficult and seemingly unfair obstacles are an inspiration to me. Hopefully, after you learn more about his journey in this book, you will be inspired to pursue and achieve your dreams too.

Congratulations Cortlan, I love you!

Your proud Mom,

Dr. Tanya Dugat Wickliff,
Professor of Engineering Practice
College of Engineering at Texas A&M University

Prologue

The title "<u>Young and Driven</u>," has two very important connections to my life.

The first reason for the title is the more straightforward interpretation of the title. It is meant to be a play on the phrase "Young & Dumb." This phrase came up during my orientation at Harvard Law School and stuck with me.

Law school orientation was a daunting experience, to say the least. We were gathered in a room with over 500 new students. Then we were told how successful everyone is; my classmates were Hollywood actors, business owners, Olympians, Rhodes Scholars, hedge fund managers, and the list goes on. The entire experience was intimidating, and largely a blur. Nevertheless, in the midst of that canned praise and daunting data, we got one word of warning, "No matter what you do from here on, you will never again be able to say that you were young and dumb."

Considering that we were starting law school and, on average, the members of the audience were about 24-25 years old, had at least one college degree, and had worked for 1-2 years, this was a reasonable statement to make. However, I personally took exception to that statement. I was barely 20 years old, and it didn't seem fair that less than 3 weeks out of my teens, I no longer could have young and dumb moments. I felt like I was being deprived of a rite of passage.

Yet, the more I thought about it, the better I felt. What does it mean to be young and dumb? It means to exist in a phase of life where you do not know what you want from life and/or how to get it. When you are young, you do reckless and illogical things, but not because you strive to be illogical—you act in objectively illogical and reckless manners because you are pursuing the wrong goals or pursuing the right goals the wrong way. Thus, being young and dumb means prioritizing short-term gains at the expense of long-term success.

With that understanding, I realized that I never want to be that kind of person. And for the majority of my life, I had not been that person. I knew what I wanted and systematically moved towards my goals. Yes, I made mistakes and even did things I later realized was idiotic— throughout this book, you will see examples of these naïve moments and bone-head mistakes. However, success is not the absence of failure, but the perseverance over it.

I am sure you have heard the adage: "Make a mistake once and it becomes a lesson; make the same mistake twice and it becomes a choice." Well, I live by a similar creed, which I hope you will adopt, that says, *"See or make a mistake once and it becomes a lesson; afterward, make that same mistake and it becomes a choice."* It is my hope that you can see the mistakes that I made, and use them as lessons to make your journey easier.

If not young and dumb; what should we be? For me, the answer has been driven! One of the benefits of being young is everything is possible because you haven't learned any differently. I am defined by my desire to pursue and achieve my "impossible" dreams regardless of what stands in my way. It is my hope that, regardless of your age—whether you are young or young at heart—you will hold onto this kind of youthful resolve and let it drive you to do extraordinary things.

The second reason for the title is a personal one. My dad was a mechanic all of my life—my time with him was inextricably linked to cars. Whether it was him teaching me how to use a buffer, us doing donuts in an old Cadillac, or racing go-karts on the dirt road in front of his shop, to be around Dad was to be around cars. Perhaps my earliest memory was sitting in his lap "steering" his truck up Parmer Lane on the way to our house. (I put "steering" in quotes because I would hope he didn't let a three-year-old kid actually take control of the wheel—although, with Dad, there is no telling.)

My dad has been a central motivating force for most of my achievements thus far and continues to inspire and motivate me today. So it seems fitting that the title of this book should have something to do with cars. Thus, the title Young and Driven pays homage to the man who both taught me how to drive and be driven.

Despite the title, this book will not be rife with driving analogies. I do not live my life a quarter-mile at a time, and a road trip did not teach me everything I need to know about life. The central theme of this book is: *Success can be achieved by anyone who is driven enough to apply unrelenting, consistent, and intentional effort to make their dreams a reality.*

Chapter 0.1:
Note to Ambitious Professionals

After writing the first edition of this book, I had the opportunity to travel around the country speaking at companies and conferences, and I talked with groups of professionals in a variety of industries. What I found was a disturbing trend of people feeling stagnant in their careers and companies.

There is nothing more enthralling and inspiring than witnessing a person pursuing their passion. The joy that you see in their face and the superhuman charisma and spirit they show in those moments is beyond explanation. Conversely, there are few things more disheartening than seeing someone wasting away while biding time between vacations. Whether you are pursuing your passion and find yourself in a rut or you are in an unfulfilling career, <u>Young</u>

and Driven can help you get back on track towards pursuing your dreams.

When reading this book, I want you to see this as a blueprint for finding and pursuing your passions. Whether your passion is progressing in your current career, finding a new career, entrepreneurship, or engaging in intrapreneurship at their company, this book is for you. While it is ultimately your responsibility to determine your passion, this book is designed to help you think critically about what you want from your career and life, and then give you the tools to attain your desires.

The name Overdrive is truly fitting for this edition—I added 80 pages of additional content designed to help you accelerate your success. I strongly recommend that professionals pay close attention to the chapters "Get the Right Team," "Learn from Mistakes: Yours and Others," and "Don't Share Your Dreams." These chapters were greatly expanded for professionals to address frequently asked questions about career advancement.

Additionally, in selecting examples to illustrate the different lessons and principles that have guided me through my academic and professional career, I sought to choose the most interesting and/or relatable illustrations. However, I and others have successfully applied all the principles in this book to academic, professional and personal pursuits. Any goal you are ambitious enough to dream, the tools, principles and exercises herein can help you attain.

Young and Driven: Overdrive is my attempt to pay it forward and deposit into others the guidance that was given to me. So please feel free to utilize the contact information in the back of the book should you have any follow-up questions or concerns. Thank you for giving me the opportunity to share with you some tips for professional and personal success.

Chapter 0.2:
Note to Driven Students

    This note is to all the students reading this book. Thank you for taking your first steps to being *young and driven scholars*. I am excited to be a part of your academic and professional journey.

    I spent over a decade traveling around the country speaking to youth and young adults at conferences, community events, high schools, and universities. In my travels, I have heard a consistently mounting frustration with the world and the way things are progressing. Your generation of youth has shared feelings of being unheard and marginalized in their classrooms, campuses, and communities. I am sure that a lot of you reading this feel the same way. I want to start by saying that *you are not alone*!

There are young people from around the world who are sick of having their voices ignored, tired of the way things are and who want to make a difference. These young people know that there are things going wrong around them but don't feel like they have the ability to create positive change. If you feel that way I want you to read this next statement closely—if you don't read anything else in this book, I want you to know: *YOU ARE ENOUGH!* You are talented enough, smart enough, beautiful enough, charismatic enough, and enough of everything you need to be in order to make a positive change in your lives, your family's lives, and the lives of all those around you!

Regardless of what you choose to pursue in life, you have in you the ability to be successful. Remember, teenagers have moved nations and college students have changed the world. There is no minimum or maximum age to find and fulfill your purpose in life. And even though you may doubt the strength of your influence, know that there are already people looking up to you—whether it is friends, family, casual acquaintances, or people you don't even know. We all have someone looking up to and emulating us. I was 7 years old looking up to an 11-year-old brother. Everyone has somebody that will follow in their footsteps; the question is: Where are you going to lead them? Down a pathway of success or destruction? The choice is yours.

This edition of <u>Young and Driven</u> is called Overdrive. In the world of cars, overdrive is the gear above a car's top gear that allows it to go faster with less energy and effort— that's what I want for all of you. I want you to all get to your dreams faster, but also for you to work smart and get there without wasting energy. To help you on your journey, I took the original <u>Young and Driven</u> book and added an extra 80 pages of exercises, explanations and answers to frequently asked questions.

This book talks heavily about academic pursuits because a *marketable* college education—degree(s) that qualifies you for numerous lucrative job opportunities immediately upon graduation—is one of the most straightforward pathways to success. However, if your passion takes you down a different pathway, this book will still provide you with the tools you need for success.

For the entrepreneurial-minded and those choosing to blaze a non-traditional trail to success, I greatly expanded the "Get the Right Team," and "Learn from Mistakes: Yours and Others." Additionally, be especially attentive to the chapters "Know What Drives You," "Establish Goals," and "Create a Plan." The exercises in those chapters will be particularly useful on your trailblazing journey.

This book is designed to grow with you in your journey. Thus, I strongly encourage you to revisit this material as you progress through academia and into your careers. And remember that, regardless of what examples I chose for a particular section, all of these tools are applicable for any pursuit. In other words, any goal you are ambitious enough to dream, the tools, principles, and exercises in this book can help you attain.

Young and Driven: Overdrive is my attempt to pay it forward and deposit into others the guidance that was given to me. So please feel free to utilize the contact information in the back of the book should you have any follow-up questions or concerns. Also, follow the social media pages for additional tips on academic and professional success. Thank you for giving me the opportunity to share some of the tips for success in your academic, personal, and professional journeys.

Chapter 1:
Introduction: Driven to Achieve

A third-grade kid does a book report on Dr. Martin Luther King, Jr. and is filled with excitement because he found out something he had never heard before: Dr. King got his PhD when he was 26 years old. He is so excited that he tells you that he is going to get a doctorate degree just like Dr. King, and he adds that he is going to get his doctorate *before* he turns 26 years old. What do you say to him? "Kids say the darndest things," you might think. Maybe you write it off the first time.

However, what do you say a year later when this kid still has it in his mind that he is going to graduate with a doctorate degree by his 26th birthday *and* he has now picked out his majors? He proudly announces that he plans to get a BS in some field of engineering, a law degree, and then maybe find an MD/ PhD program to finally achieve the title of Doctor. Do you tell him that he can't do it? That might be too harsh. Instead, do you just let him know that in order to accomplish this goal, he would have to start college no later than the age of 15?

What do you say six years later, when at the age of 14, he is actually applying to college? How would you advise him five years after that, when he is graduating with his BS in Bioengineering from Rice University at the age of 19? Now he is the youngest engineer in the nation, but he's still pushing towards a bigger dream. Would you think that was possible? Would you be convinced when three years after that, he graduates from Harvard Law School with his JD at the age of 22 as one of the youngest black law school graduates in the school's more-than-200-year history? Do you know what you would say six months later when he is admitted to the State Bar of Texas as the youngest of more than 94,000 attorneys in the state? And at the same time, he's completing his first semester in a PhD program. Can you imagine the elation he felt two-and-a-half years after that when he was only 26 days away from receiving his PhD in Engineering and simultaneously 30 days away from his 26th birthday? Would that be hard to imagine?

I am that kid! Starting in the third grade, I spent almost 20 years working towards the same goal: I was going to become Dr. Wickliff at a younger age than Dr. King graduated with his doctorate. During the pursuit of my goal, I have been called a dreamer, unrealistic, naïve, immature, uninformed, ignorant, childish, and a lot of other synonyms I've tried to forget. This name-calling came from all different directions—it came from people who were old, young, near-and-dear, and relative strangers. Some of the discouragement was even well-intentioned, from people who were trying to get me to realize that I was pursuing what they believed to be an unattainable pipe dream. It would be a lie to tell you I didn't spend several nights lying awake thinking the same thing, especially during the difficult times. However, less than a month away from achieving what many thought was unachievable, a dream that had been 18 years in the making, people finally stopped telling me how impossible my dream was. Eventually, people started asking me how and why I did it.

When asked why, I have given a lot of reasons: I wanted the title of Doctor, I wanted to have as many career options as possible, I was (and still am) genuinely interested in all of my chosen fields, I wanted to be qualified for jobs with high levels of responsibility, etc. All of that was true. Yet none of those reasons are what got me through 11 years of all-nighters in college and years of early morning meetings and late work days. Although I have always been greatly inspired by the example of Dr. King, my greatest motivation was given to me by another man in October of 2000.

I did not know it at the time, but early that month, I would have my last face-to-face conversation with my dad, Anthony "Tony" Wickliff. I vividly remember coming outside of my family's church in Liberty, Texas to see my dad leaning against his pickup truck. We talked a bit about school, and then, out of nowhere, he said, "Son, when you get rich and famous, I only want one thing."

"Of course, Dad! What is it?"

He responded, "Buy me a Corvette."

My dad had been a mechanic for most of my life, and it wasn't just his occupation—it was his true passion. He had worked his way up from being a volunteer mechanic to owning his own auto body, paint, and mechanic shop. His hands and forearms were always a few shades darker than the rest of his body because of a layer of engine grease that just never seemed to disappear. In fact, he seemed to have oil stains on everything he owned, from his jeans and t-shirts to his Sunday best. This was because there was never a time when he wouldn't fix a car for someone. On more than one occasion, he had even resurrected a car in a church parking lot. That level of dedication to your craft can only come from having a true love and passion for what you do.

I know unequivocally that my dad had a passion for cars. For that reason, I am thankful he never had to find out how little his ten-year-old son knew about cars, because I think I would have made him feel somewhat embarrassed. When he asked me for a Corvette, I had no idea what it was, so I naïvely responded, "How about I get you a Ferrari or a—"

Before I could finish the sentence and suggest a Hummer or a Range Rover or some other car I had seen in a movie, Dad interrupted me and said, "Stop acting like your mom, always trying to tell me what's best for me." He chuckled in his comical, unique way and declared, "I want a Corvette."

In that moment, I promised my dad that I would become successful enough to buy him a new Corvette. Because I had never seen the sticker price of his dream car, I had no idea the level of success I was committing to achieving.

That promise stuck with me, because less than a week later, my dad died from a heart attack. Just as vividly as I remember my dad leaning against his pickup truck and asking me for a Corvette, I remember opening my front door to find my mom standing in the middle of the living room, crying, when I got home from school. There are few things more devastating to anyone—let alone a ten-year-old boy—than talking to someone you love before going to bed and then finding out he died a few hours later in his sleep. What hurt even worse was finding out that when he had gone to the doctor to get checked out earlier that month, he couldn't afford any of the diagnostic and preventative care that might have saved his life. That kind of hurt never fully goes away. However, it doesn't have to derail you, and if you work at it, you can find a way to let those feelings drive you. And that is what I did.

See, the more I learned about Corvettes, the more I realized the level of faith my dad had placed in me. Dad was from a farming/ranching family and had been raised on handshake deals and cash businesses. This meant that every automobile part he ordered, every tool he owned, and every car he bought was bought with cash. One day, while reflecting on my dad's death, it dawned on me that in his mind, he fully expected his ten-year-old son to become the type of man who would someday be able to buy him a brand-new Corvette—in cash. Wow!

Why he thought that and what he was expecting me to accomplish, I will never know. The best I can figure is that he must have believed that naïve third-grader who had told him these outlandish dreams three years earlier. He must have fully expected that the type of person who could pull that off would be able to get him his dream car, too.

> "What counts is not necessarily the size of the dog in the fight – it's the size of the fight in the dog."
> Pres. Dwight D. Eisenhower

It became my personal mission to live up to the potential Dad had seen in me. However, it wasn't just to make my dad proud or to one day be able to own an excellent piece of American muscle in honor of him, although those were definitely motivators. To remain vigilant, I needed a personal motivation.

That motivation was wanting to become the man Dad had envisioned, because that kind of person would have the ability to take care of the people I love. I could help ensure the people I love would have access to the medical care they needed—I would never have to bury a loved one for the need of a few extra dollars. Avoiding that hurt is the real reason I have pursued and continue to pursue my dreams with such passion. I know that I have not yet fully become the person that I believe Dad expected me to become, but 26 days after first writing these words, I took one giant step closer to that ideal when I walked across the stage and accepted my PhD in engineering.

But my insatiable drive to pursue my passions did not stop with that last trip across the graduation stage. Since then, I have traveled the world encouraging people of all ages to pursue their passion. I continue to pursue excellence in the legal profession and as a member of my university's faculty and staff. My business clients span numerous industries, and I consistently find myself setting records in my professional life as well.

This chapter has shown you a bit about what ignited my personal drive to achieve professionally and academically. It is my sincere belief and experience that: *Success can be achieved by anyone who is driven enough to apply unrelenting, consistent, and intentional effort to make their dreams a reality.* The question becomes "How?" How did *I* turn my drive into achievement, and more importantly, how can *you*? That question is what this book will address.

Although I will be sharing stories and experiences from my life, this is not an autobiography. This book will present the concrete steps that I took and that I would recommend to anybody who is trying to pursue an ambitious dream. I have successfully applied these techniques to my academic, personal, and professional dreams. Whether you are pursuing academic excellence, success at your job, team achievement, a new career, some form of personal growth or fitness goals, or taking that first leap into entrepreneurship, the steps to success never really change.

Journey with me in the pages that follow, and you too can build lasting accomplishments and make your dreams a reality.

Chapter 2:
Believe

All great accomplishments start with your belief; if you do not believe that something is possible, you will not sincerely pursue it. You have to believe in something before you can do it. Therefore, belief is where we will start.

Regardless of what dream you are pursuing, achieving any major accomplishment in life is like constructing a new building. People talk about having a good foundation as the start of any major project. However, any experienced contractor/builder knows that the construction process begins long before you pour the foundation of a building. Any great building starts with some great groundwork (i.e., choosing where you want to build and preparing the ground for construction). Before you can lay a foundation or put up a frame, you have to have a ground that is suitable to build upon.

Belief is the ground on which the foundation for achievement can be laid. I think that the Biblical passage Matthew 7:24-27 says it best:

> *"Therefore everyone who hears these words of mine and puts them into practice is like a wise man who built his house on the rock. The rain came down, the streams rose, and the winds blew and beat against that house; yet it did not fall, because it had its foundation on the rock. But everyone who hears these words of mine and does not put them into practice is like a foolish man who built his house on sand. The rain came down, the streams rose, and the winds blew and beat against that house, and it fell with a great crash."*

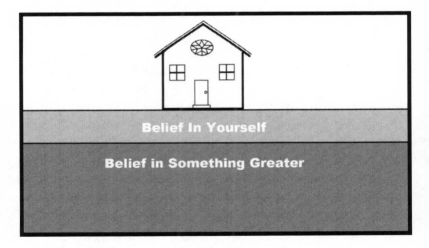

I use this parable to illustrate the idea that belief is more fundamental than the foundation. Belief is the solid ground that anchors your efforts against adversity. If you do not believe in what you are doing or do not believe that your accomplishments are possible, then when the storms of life approach, your efforts will crumble and you will give up. Rarely do we succeed the first time, every time. In order to be successful, a person often must try again and again in the face of consistent failure. However, if you do not believe that you can actually accomplish a task, you will take those initial failures as confirmation that the task is impossible and you will not try as hard or as often as you otherwise would. Therefore, without solid belief, you will never be able to build towards any significant accomplishments.

> "It ain't about how hard you hit, it's about how hard you can get hit and keep moving forward."
> Rocky Balboa
> (*Rocky Balboa*)

As in the parable, imagine building a structure. Underneath that structure is your belief. Much like the ground has multiple layers, so too does your belief. There are two primary levels of belief that are paramount for success: belief in yourself, which is the ground closest to the surface, and belief in something greater than yourself, which makes up the deeper bedrock.

We will start with the surface (i.e., belief in yourself). No matter how strong and resilient the bedrock you build upon is, if you do not have solid ground above it, your foundation can shift and your building can crumble. Similarly, no matter how deep your faith is in something greater than yourself (e.g., family, God, country, laws, karma, etc.), having a solid belief in yourself is still paramount for building any lasting accomplishments.

Belief In Something Greater

> "Let us remember: One book, one pen, one child, and one teacher can change the world"
> Malala Yousafzai

Belief in yourself is often the hardest part of anyone's journey, and in several areas of your life, it will become a daily struggle. We are constantly bombarded with the idea that we are not enough to accomplish our goals.

Sometimes your circumstances tell you that you are not enough to accomplish your goals. You may be competing with people who have more resources than you, and more access to opportunities than you. Or you may feel discouraged because you know of people who had so many advantages over you yet failed to accomplish what you are seeking to achieve. None of that matters!

Your past tragedies don't dictate your future trajectory. What that means is that where you start does not determine where you end. History is filled with people who had humble beginnings and yet overcame the statistics and beat the odds to do extraordinary things. There is nothing that separates them from anyone else, including you, other than their belief in themselves and their willingness to persevere.

Another way in which we are told that we are not good enough is that the people around us explicitly tell us that we cannot achieve extraordinary things. No matter where you are or what you have previously accomplishment, some people are going to make the baseless assumption that you cannot achieve. I'll use myself as an example.

At 19 years old, I was about to be the youngest engineer in the nation, was graduating from the best bioengineering program in Texas, had founded several national recognized initiatives, had completed research in several disciplines, and had accomplished a great deal both academically and professionally. I was clearly ready for the next step in my academic journey, law school. I vividly remember sitting across the desk from our university's pre-law advisor. I excitedly told him my aspirations, shared my transcript, and told him the schools I wanted to apply to. His first response was to tell me that I was aiming too high. He told me that, despite all of my accomplishments to that point, I needed to apply to lower-ranked schools if I wanted to go to law school.

Clearly, he was wrong: seven months later, I got accepted into Harvard Law School, one of the top-ranked law schools in the nation. Three years later, I graduated and became the youngest licensed attorney in Texas. However, looking back, 19-year-old me couldn't see into the future, and having someone with over a decade of academic advising experience tell me "You are aiming too high" was jarring. I had to make the decision to believe in myself more than I believed in that pre-law advisor's opinion.

That person was an example of someone who honestly didn't have my best interests at heart, but not everyone who "puts you down" falls into that same category. Sometimes the people telling you what you can't do are well-intentioned family members, friends, and trusted advisors who are just concerned that you are setting yourself up for failure by being unrealistic. Often, these are people who have experienced the heartache and dejection that is associated with failure, and they don't want you to feel the same pain.

Nevertheless, it doesn't matter what people and circumstances tell you is possible—the only thing that matters is what *you* believe is possible. However, the problem is that we ourselves are oftentimes our worst critic.

The fact of the matter is that despite all of the songs, memes, parables, and popular cultural sayings that tell us to "shake [our] haters off," oftentimes we are our own biggest naysayers. *You* will tell yourself you can't accomplish a goal before you ever hear it from someone else. Elena Delle Donne said it best: "There's nobody who talks to you in a day more than yourself." So no matter how encouraging other people may be, if you aren't able to honestly tell yourself that you will succeed, your personal naysaying will drown out every other voice. There is no way that you will be successful if that happens.

> "No one has a perfect life. Everybody has something that they wish was not the way it is."
> Stan Lee

"Believe in yourself!" This is easy to say but hard to do. The first step in the process is to stop putting other people on a pedestal. Often, the reason you don't believe in yourself is because you elevate other people above you. We look at other people as having some "it factor" that we lack, or some understanding of the world that we don't get. Instead of saying somebody did better than us on a test because they studied harder or a teammate beat us out for a starting position because they trained harder, our first assumption is that they are smarter or better than we are.

But here's the thing: there is nobody on Earth that is born better than you. We all come into the world the same way: crying and naked. There will come times in your life when others are ahead of you, yes, but you possess the ability to make a change whenever you want. One of the greatest gifts of humanity is the ability to choose to evolve. However, nothing will change unless you believe it is possible.

Next, know what you are good at and stop faulting yourself for not being the best at everything. When talking with people around the world, I've noticed that we all have the tendency to hone in on the things somebody else can do that we cannot. For example, if a person is not particularly good with math, then they will be awestruck by anyone who is exceptional at math and will assume that, that specific ability is a sign of their overall superior intelligence. In that context, we assume the other person is better than us because they excel at one of the skills we lack. We essentially assume the stuff we are good at is easy for everyone because it is easy for us. Unconsciously, you are telling yourself that your talent is not a talent and that you would be a success, too, if you just had what the other person possesses.

> "I was never top of the class at school, but my classmates must have seen potential in me, because my nickname was 'Einstein.'"
> Dr. Stephen Hawking

However, it has also been my experience that, most of the time, the other person is doing the same thing—they are looking at the things *you* can do that they cannot and saying you must be smarter or better than *them*. Returning to the previous example, maybe you aren't proficient in math, but you have a more extensive vocabulary and excel at writing. The person who excels at math may very well be envious of your talent in language arts classes. We all have a tendency to minimize ourselves and our abilities; resist the temptation to do so! Recognize what you are good at and understand and accept that that will not include everything.

> "Don't envy someone else's gift. Discover your own."
> Tavis Smiley

I excel at problem-solving and reasoning. I am confident in saying there is nobody I personally know who is better at looking at real-world problems and creating solutions. With that being said, I am a horribly slow sprinter. I literally know dozens of friends and family members who can run a 40-yard dash or 100-meter sprint faster than me. In high school, my first girlfriend bench-pressed more than me, and it wasn't even a substantial amount. There is literally a laundry list of things that other people do or have done better than me. I am a good cook, but a lot of my family and friends cook better. I am a horrible artist, a third-row tenor in the choir, a below-average mechanic, a subpar farmer, a mediocre basketball player, inept at driving a stick shift, a horrible rancher, incompetent in heat transfer equations, and the list goes on. I want you to see this list, because there was some point in my life that one or more of my peers excelled in each of these areas. But regardless of who was stronger or faster than me, who could dunk on me, or who got a better grade than me in school, I know that I am still, and have always been, a great problem-solver.

Ultimately, my problem-solving ability is how I make a living, and it's what I use to support those around me. And by fully embracing my talent, I am able to do things I never dreamed would be possible. For example, despite my love of art & music, I never learned how to paint particularly well and am a mediocre musician. However, because of my problem-solving ability, the artists I know come to me for help with solving issues with contracts, sampling agreements, venues, vendors, and supply chains (i.e., getting things to them and to their customers quickly). Thus, even though I never became a great artist, through my problem-solving ability I still help bring great art into the world. Remember to be flexible in your approach to achieving your dreams.

The last step to help you more confidently believe in yourself is to remember that another's success does not diminish you. We are often taught that winning is a zero-sum game, which means that in order for you to win, someone else must lose. This is something that is ingrained in us through sports and competitions at an early age. We grow up with ideas like, "If I want the big prize, I need to make sure that nobody else gets it." Or we are taught to think, "If I want to be the champion, everyone else has to lose."

In the real world, that is not the case. It is entirely possible for two individuals to be highly successful simultaneously without negatively impacting each other. Resist the temptation to feel that seeing a successful person will somehow diminish the odds that *you* can be successful. If you do not, then seeing someone extraordinary is going to be disheartening, because you will unconsciously think you need to be better than them to be a success. Remember that, outside of the very specific context where your goals involve winning competitions, you don't ever need to beat anyone else to succeed.

Practically speaking, it is easy to say these things but hard to do them; here is an exercise that can help you build confidence in your ability:

EXERCISE 1: DAILY AFFIRMATIONS

1. Come up with three positive statements about yourself that you absolutely know to be true (i.e., your confident phrases). For example, if you know

you are Picasso reincarnated, make your statement "I am a great artist." If you are the strongest person at your school, say "I am extremely strong."

2. Come up with two statements you want to be true but aren't as confident about (i.e., your aspirational phrases). Maybe you are a great artist but you are working on your business skill set, in which case, you can say, "I am a successful business owner." If you are a superstar athlete who isn't as confident about your day job, your statement could be, "I am a superstar employee."

3. Once you have picked your five phrases (three confident phrases and two aspirational phrases), do this step daily.
   a. Every morning when you wake up and every evening before you go to bed, repeat those phrases three times.
   b. Additionally, any time you start to doubt yourself, say all five phrases out loud (or in your mind if you are in mixed company).

4. As you build confidence, periodically update your aspirational phrases to new things you want to improve on.

For me, I had been told most of my life that I was smart, so it didn't take me much to believe that "I am smart." I have been tutoring people since I was in the third grade; so I already knew "I am a great tutor." Finally, whether it is a word problem or a real-world scenario, I have always excelled at finding simple solutions to complex problems; so I knew "I am a great problem-solver." Those were my three positive statements I knew to be true.

In spite of my confidence in my intelligence, I had set some lofty goals in life. In order for me to believe that I could accomplish them, my first aspirational phrase was "I can do anything I put my mind to." Another area where I wasn't as confident as I would have liked to be was in physical activities. As I previously stated, I wasn't

> "Once you replace negative thoughts with positive ones, you'll start having positive results."
> Willie Nelson

exactly the strongest or fastest in high school. Still, I recognized that a lot of my goals were going to take time, time that I would only have if I lived a long and healthy life. Therefore, physical fitness would be important for my long-term success, so my next aspirational phrase was simply "I am a beast." Note that these phrases are for you and you alone—don't worry about whether other people get them or not. For me, "I am a beast" meant that I had the physical endurance, strength, and stamina to do that last rep or push through that last 100 meters. As such, I didn't have an excuse to quit.

In addition to this verbal affirmation exercise, try what my mom fondly called "fake it 'til you make it." Within reason, in your daily life, try to act in the manner you would if your aspirational statements were already true. The "within reason" part is particularly important! This is not a license to perpetrate and live outside of your means, nor should you put yourself or anyone else in harm's way. This exercise is an opportunity for you to push yourself and deepen your resolve. If your statement is "I am a great doctor," try attending a medical seminar or writing an article for a medical journal. If your statement is "I am the best employee at my company," try showing up an extra 15 minutes early to work. The goal is to emulate the successful behaviors of the person you want to be until you become that person.

For me, when I was working on my confidence and telling myself, "I can do anything I put my mind to," I picked up extra assignments at work. Thus, I would dedicate some time during the workweek to a project that was a bit outside of my expertise or perceived skill set. This meant that sometimes I was a bioengineer working on an electrical engineering problem and sometimes I was a lawyer working on an HR issue. As I experienced success in areas I had never believed I could excel in, it gradually made me more and more confident when saying, "I can do anything I put my mind to."

Do this continuously until you believe the last two aspirational phrases as strongly as you believe the first three. When that happens, pick new aspirational phrases and repeat the process.

> "I found that every time I asked permission, the answer tended to be no, so I had to make my own yeses."
> Issa Rae

Note that properly embodying the concept of "fake it 'til you make it" can be a powerful tool for your long-term success regardless of what you pursue. If you are not willing to do at least as much as those who have achieved what *you* hope to accomplish, you will not succeed.

Establishing a strong, solid belief in yourself is a significant step towards being able to achieve. Still, for me and for most people, it isn't enough!

No matter how confident you are in yourself, there will always be something that sets you back. It could be anything from experiencing rejection from a person you like to getting a bad evaluation or being passed over for a promotion. Life always finds a way to "chin-check" you, challenge your confidence, and test your resolve. When that happens, if you only have a solid surface belief in yourself without a deeper belief in something greater than yourself, then you become susceptible to unexpected "sinkholes" in your confidence.

Sinkholes occur when the bedrock underneath a structure is missing or erodes. This can happen for any number of reasons. Once it does, the absence or weakening of the underlying bedrock puts a lot of strain on the surface material. If there is anything heavy on the surface, the surface layer of the ground will buckle and a sinkhole will form, destroying the surface structure. Even though a bedrock may take years to erode, these sinkholes can form quickly and without warning.

Put a little differently, a sinkhole forms when there is nothing holding up the top layer that a building's foundation rests upon. Eventually, the top layer stops being able to hold up the building and everything comes crashing down. The bigger/heavier the building becomes, the more likely it is to fall through an unsupported top layer.

In our analogy, your belief in yourself is the top layer of the ground, and your belief in something greater than yourself is the bedrock. The bigger your goals are, the more pressure you can feel if you are relying solely on your belief in yourself to support your goals. In the context of experiencing a setback, your belief in yourself can crack and crumble, and if there is no greater belief supporting your self-confidence, then sinkholes can abruptly form.

Sinkholes are situations where your belief in yourself collapses under the pressure of what you are trying to accomplish. These situations can derail your progression towards your goals. However, sinkholes can be avoided by finding something greater than yourself to believe in and then maintaining that belief.

A belief in something greater acts as a bedrock that props up your confidence. This additional support is something you can fall back on as you strive to build towards your dreams. Regardless of how confident you are in yourself, your belief is going to be shaken from time to time. In those moments, it is paramount for you to believe in and be pushed by something greater than you.

> "If you give up at the first sign of struggle, you're really not ready to be successful."
> Kevin Hart

The easiest example of belief in something greater than yourself that can push you forward is faith in God. For me, my Christianity, my belief in Jesus, and my faith in God are significant reasons for why I am where I am today. In my life, I have had numerous setbacks that could have easily halted my progress; in some cases, they came very close. For example, during my last two years at Harvard Law School, both of my grandfathers, my great aunt who was like a grandmother to me, and my great-uncle who inspired me to attend law school all died. The belief that "…in all things God works for the good of those who love him, who have been called according to his purpose" (Rom 8:28) sustained me through trying times. In times when I was sad or angry and when things did not go the way I wanted them to, I could fall back on the belief that somehow everything was going to work out for the best.

Furthermore, this belief in God pushed me to do more than I had previously thought was possible. If I believe that "I can do all things through Christ who strengthens me" (Phil. 4:13), then that includes meeting aggressive work deadlines and acing multiple midterms in one week.

I've had my fair share of confidence-shaking moments—whether it was the first time I unambiguously failed an exam, the multiple times I fried a circuit board, my numerous rejected job applications, my failed relationships, or just the days when I didn't see the positive impact of all of my hard work, I have had my belief in myself challenged on numerous occasions. Any time my self-assurance waned and my confidence failed me, I was able to get through because of my personal belief in God.

My Christian faith is the belief that works for me; it may not be what works for you. However, in order to accomplish great things in life, you must believe in something. Even though faith in God is a great belief to have and I would personally recommend Christianity to anyone, it is not the only belief that can push you to new heights. There are three requirements for a belief to be a basis upon which you can build significant accomplishments: the belief must be 1. *Comforting*, 2. *Inspiring*, and 3. *Believable*.

> "I was taught that you must believe in something greater than yourself to get something bigger than yourself."
> James Prince

In order for a belief in something greater than yourself to actually help support your accomplishments, it must be something that comforts you in times of distress and turmoil. The mental strain of aspiring to something extraordinary can already be intense. However, if you add to that a traumatic experience (e.g., the death of a loved one, a major failure, financial hardships, etc.), it can become impossible to keep your sanity and joy. In moments like that, your belief must comfort you.

In addition to comforting you, a belief must be inspirational. Your faith should tell you that you have potential beyond measure and should inspire you to believe in your ability to achieve great things. The goal is for your confidence in your faith to bolster your confidence and belief in your ability to accomplish your goals. For example, let's say you believe in the power and spirit of your ancestors. They are a part of you, so some of their greatness can be found in you. This is an inspirational belief, because increasing your confidence in those ancestors increases your confidence in your inherited genetics. Thus, your belief in them will inspire you to believe that *you* have extraordinary capabilities within *you*.

The final aspect of an impactful and supportive faith is that the belief must be believable. This doesn't mean that everyone must believe it or that anyone else must find it plausible—this only requires that *you* must really believe in it. So don't pick something you consider to be far-fetched or unrealistic. This also means that a truly beneficial belief in something greater than yourself cannot just be inherited traditions. Put simply, your grandparent's faith won't sustain you!

A reoccurring theme in this book is that success and achieving your dreams is a personal journey. As such, the ideas, wishes, believes, dreams, and ambitions of others are not something that can sustain you. You must find your personal reasons and methods for how and why you achieve success. However, you *can* believe the same thing that your family believes (my family has been Christian for generations). At some point on your journey, though, you just have to find your own personal reason for your beliefs. My faith is my faith; even though I believe in the same things that so many of my family members do, I sometimes believe for drastically different reasons than the rest of my family does.

With these three requirements in mind, what are some examples of belief in something greater than yourself outside of religion? Family is a good example. If you come from a strong and proud family, it could be the belief that strength and excellence are hardwired into your DNA. Thus, any setback that occurs is just a temporary setback that you will easily overcome. You could believe in Karma and that the arc of the world bends towards justice for those who are just. If you are a police officer or career military, you could believe in the sanctity of your brotherhood and hold true to the ideals of your organization. Other examples include believing in your country or state constitution and believing that the sanctity and necessity of enforcing and abiding by the laws of the land is a way to maintain equality and justice.

Your confidence can be supported by any belief that is greater than yourself as long as it gives you comfort, inspires you to push past your limits, and is something you deem believable.

In the words of Shepherd Book, "I don't care what you believe in, just believe in it."

When you have a solid belief in yourself paired with a strong belief in something greater than yourself, you are ready to start building towards something exceptional.

Chapter 3:
Know What Drives You

If belief is the ground upon which your accomplishments are built, knowing what drives you is the foundation. I also like to call this "Knowing Your 'Why.'" I call it this because knowing what drives you (i.e., your motivations) is knowing why you are willing to work harder, why you are willing to push further, and why you will not quit. This is you establishing a motivation or motivations that can act as a driving force to push you when everything else tells you to give up.

I will not tell you it is impossible to achieve success in life without knowing what drives you and establishing solid motivations, but it is difficult. Using our surface/bedrock analogy, there are numerous structures that can be built without a solid foundation: tents, trailer homes, sheds, shacks, and even some small buildings are all successfully built without a strong foundation. However, most structures built without a solid foundation are more temporary, smaller, and more fragile. As such, when a builder fails to establish a strong foundation for a structure, they are limited in the scope of what they can build.

Similarly, if you fail to establish your foundational core motivations, you limit the height and magnitude of what you can achieve. Imposing towers and magnificent monuments that stand the test of time are not built (and cannot be built) without solid foundations. Thus, as in the metaphor, the accomplishments you seek to build without a firm understanding of what drives you will be shorter-lived and smaller.

In other words, nobody haphazardly breaks world records or nonchalantly achieves where so many others have failed. Simply put, if it were easy, everyone would do it. So, if you want to do what has never been done, you must be motivated as nobody has ever been motivated before.

> *"... about half of what separates the successful entrepreneurs from the non-successful ones is pure perseverance."*
> Steve Jobs

Achieving greatness requires you to find the type of motivation that will push you harder than everyone else. You must find that thought that will drive you to persevere. This should be the thing that can make you jump out of bed in the morning and the thing that makes it harder to go to sleep at night. Ultimately, the right motivation can make the impossible possible.

How do you find the right motivation for your particular journey? The first thing to realize about your motivations is that they are not dependent on your journey or the course of action you choose. A lot of the time, people chose what they are going to do and *then* think of a "motivation." This is not a motivation; this is a justification for doing something you already plan to do.

The problem with operating this way is that it will leave you oblivious to alternative courses of action that might better serve your needs and desires. When you choose something and then decide why you chose it, there is a strong tendency to tailor your answers to fit the situation. A good example of this concept can be found in romantic relationships.

A long-term relationship is hard work, and you need to have some consistent and strong motivation to keep putting in that work on a daily basis. And, to be candid, you are far more motivated to work on a relationship when the other person has the traits you desire and/or need. In my experience, the strongest relationships are established when people have taken the time to think critically about what they are looking for in a significant other (i.e., "why" they want to date someone) and then find the person who matches those needs/desires. This way, they can critically evaluate whether someone does or does not address all of their key "I-care-abouts" and be motivated to work harder when a person does meet those requirements.

Conversely, I know several people who decided whom they wanted to date first and then thought of why they wanted to date that person. As previously stated, this pattern of thinking has a tendency to make you tailor your supposed desires/needs to match the person rather than selecting a person who matches your needs to begin with. The problem with this scenario is that it doesn't force (or allow) you to think critically about whether the relationship is actually addressing your long-term needs or if it is just based on a flimsy short-term desire (e.g., you're lonely, they look good, you're afraid, etc.). Consequently, most of these relationships did not last, because one or both people weren't motivated to continue.

Why did I use a relationship example to illustrate this point? First, I wanted to have a good opportunity to state that whom you choose as a partner/spouse is the single greatest determinate of your success next to whom/what you choose to believe in. A great spouse/significant-other can provide you with the type of motivation and support that pushes you to never-before-imagined heights, whereas a bad spouse/significant-other can destroy your life. As such, I strongly encourage you to think critically and methodically about your selections.

However, the primary reason I used a relationship example is because your relationships with your goals will oftentimes be some of the longest and most involved relationships in your life. Your goals will define you and change you for the better or for the worse. I had pursued the same goal for almost two decades, and there are other goals I have pursued longer than that. Knowing that this is something that will be with you for large segments of your life (if not your entire life), you should think critically and be methodical about how you choose your goals. And much like a relationship with a person, a successful relationship with your goals is going to require you to consistently be motivated to work. Thus, I have found that it is more effective to identify your core motivations (e.g., establish your strong foundation) before you start working towards your goals.

Take an introspective look at yourself to figure out what drives you and then use that motivation to choose the goals you want to pursue. Whether you love to win, help people, protect loved ones, have excess, or simply hate failure, once you truly and honestly accept

> "I am made exactly the way I was meant to be made..."
> Megan Rapinoe

yourself for who you are, you can push yourself towards extraordinary accomplishments.

H.I.P. Motivations!

H : **HONEST**

I : **INSPIRATIONAL**

P : **PERSONAL**

The second thing to realize about your motivations is that anything can be a motivation. For some people, it is as simple as wanting to be able to attract a pretty girl or a handsome guy. For others, their motivations are as big as wanting to rid the world of injustice. Your motivation can be to earn a title of the best of the best, to beat somebody in a competition, or to never be hungry again. Any desire or past experience has the potential to be a motivator that drives you to achieve your goals.

When you are choosing your core motivations, remember the phrase "Be H.I.P." This is an acronym that captures the only three rules to abide by when choosing the core motivation you'll build your accomplishments on top of: 1. *be Honest*, 2. *be Inspirational*, and 3. *be Personal*.

Be honest with yourself! I want to lead here with the biggest mistake people make when listing motivations: they lie to themselves. Nobody else has to know what motivates you, so you gain nothing from lying other than a weak foundation to build upon. Not everyone will be motivated by pleasing God; in fact, most people won't be motivated by such an abstract target. Nor will everybody be motivated by an innate desire to help people, a love for the arts, or a love of the game. Don't lie to yourself and pretend that those are really your core motivations for success if they aren't.

I am not saying that you cannot be motivated by things outside of yourself. I had a friend in undergrad who was absolutely going to be a doctor. Yes, he wanted to help people, and yes, he wanted to have money, but that was not the foundation for his decision to become a doctor—his primary reason for wanting to become a doctor was an unyielding desire to have the knowledge and resources necessary to take care of his parents should they ever become ill. That motivation saw him through every all-nighter, every cram session, and every challenge, and I now have to address him as "Doctor."

There is no telling where you will find motivation. You may want to change the world or raise a family that never knows the pangs of true hunger. Your motivation could be the simple desire to prove your capabilities. Whatever your motivation is, acknowledge it, accept it, and be honest about it.

> "The worst lies are the ones we tell ourselves."
> Bryant McGill

Again, make sure that you are not determining your motivations based on your chosen path. We are all taught the politically correct or socially acceptable answers for why we should want to pursue a particular profession. We know them even if we aren't in the profession ourselves: *athletes are supposed to love the game/sport, doctors are supposed to want to help people, lawyers are supposed to want justice, etc.* Yes, you can still give those politically correct answers when asked in public (because they are motivators even if they are not your personal core motivators), but you still need to dig deeper to determine your actual, honest motivations.

The reason you must be honest with yourself is that the motivation you choose will be the foundation upon which you lay your goals, and goals that are not well-supported by this foundation will likely fall apart. Think of the example of hearing about a promotion into management at a company. A qualified employee decides to go for the promotion because they tell themselves, "I want the additional responsibility and challenge of management." This is great, and if they are truly motivated by that desire for responsibility and new challenges, a qualified candidate will likely succeed in this new job. However, what if this was just their politically correct answer? What if their honest motivation for wanting the job was that they are competitive and didn't want other employees to pass them up? If they do actually land that promotion, what will likely happen?

To answer this question, you must first realize that the employee in this example did not actually want a new job and definitely didn't want the new responsibilities and challenges associated with a promotion—the employee really just wanted to prove they could win when competing for the promotion. Thus, the only goal that was grounded in a core motivation was beating their coworkers out for the job. Although they might be highly motivated to successfully get the job, what will happen after they are promoted?

The goal of being a high-quality manager is not supported by their motivation. The employee-turned-manager has already beaten out his coworkers. Unless there is another core motivation driving this new manager, they will have little to no real motivation to achieve the goal of being an exceptional manager. Thus, this employee will likely be subpar at their new job.

The problem does not stop there. Think about building a house; if part of the house is not supported by the foundation, that part is more likely to shift and eventually fall apart. Imagine if a corner of a house did fall. The corner not supported by the foundation is still connected to the other portions of the house that are fixed to the foundation. Therefore, there is a good chance that other parts of the house will also fall or be significantly damaged. Similarly, when a goal that is not supported by your true motivation falls apart, it may delay or destroy your progress towards other goals. To get the promotion, the employee from our example was clearly above-average at their original job. However, now this employee has become a subpar manager. If the company decides to demote the employee back to where they began, the employee won't be worse off. But what happens if the employee is fired instead? That raises the possibility of erasing years of working towards retirement, and the loss of income could have a strong negative impact on other goals that the employee had been working towards.

Put simply, lying to yourself about your true motivations hurts you. It causes you to waste time, money, and energy pursuing things that put you further from where you want to be in life. Therefore, be honest with yourself when you are identifying your motivations.

Next, when choosing your core motivations, they must be inspiring. This means that whatever motivation you choose must actually make you want to work harder. It has to be that thing that makes you put in an extra hour on your presentation, try again & again, or proofread your work one more time.

> "Follow your heart. Don't follow what you've been told you're supposed to do."
> Jermaine Cole

When I was young, my mom coined the phrase, "We are all motivated by crap or cravings—which one is it for you?" The premise of her question is that everybody who has done anything worthwhile has been motivated by either wanting to avoid something traumatic ("Crap") or pursuing something desirable ("Cravings"). Most of the greatest athletes will tell you that they were pushed to greatness by a tough loss in their youth or by the desire to provide for their family. A lot of the greatest American success stories began with epic failures or lofty aspirations. There isn't a "right" or "wrong" type of motivation as long as it inspires you.

What are some concrete examples of motivators? Let's start with cravings. If you are a gearhead like my dad was, then you could be motivated by a car you always wanted to own. He would work hard to have extra time and money to dedicate to restoring a totaled Corvette he had acquired. That craving pushed him to get more work done.

Or maybe you are like me and have expensive taste buds. My favorite food is crabs, especially snow crabs, and I could ramble on like Benjamin Buford Blue about all the ways I like them prepared. (You have not lived until you have had some well-fried blue crabs or some perfectly prepared honey-BBQ snow crabs!) Growing up, whenever I brought home straight A's or won a competition, my parents would make me a few clusters of crabs. That was definitely a motivator for me to do well in school growing up.

Still, I tend to be motivated best by crap rather than cravings. This means that some of my strongest core motivations are avoiding things I don't like. For example, I have spent most of my life hearing people tell me what I couldn't do. No matter how many times I succeeded or defied the odds, somebody was always there waiting to tell me I should set my sights lower. This unsolicited advice was always given with a condescending look of satisfaction. They seemed proud that they had done the good deed of saving me from the disappointment of my inevitable failure. That grated on me so much! Any time

that happened, I became determined that I never wanted to
see the look of satisfaction on their face from having been
proved right. That motivation got me through several all-
nighters and pushed me to achieve things I didn't know I
could.

Ultimately, some of the greatest motivators in life will
come from potentially traumatic circumstances. None of
the motivators I mentioned in the previous paragraphs had
as profound an impact on me as the passing of my father.
There is never a good time to lose a parent, but the timing
of Dad's death was especially difficult. Two months before
his passing and with his support, my mom had quit her job
to pursue her doctorate. Thus, not only was there the hurt of
Dad passing, but there was also the aftermath of growing
up poorer in a single-parent household for the rest of my
childhood. During that time, there were so many things I
couldn't have that I wanted and so many experiences I
never wanted to live through again. As a result, the tragedy
of my dad's death fueled me more than any snow crabs or
condescending teacher ever could.

Just because you endure a
traumatic experience does not
mean that it has to limit you or
slow you down. We are all faced
with tough circumstances that are
outside of our control. These
challenges can be things like
growing up without much money,
personal health challenges,
instability in the household, caring
for a sick family member, or even
the death of someone close to you. The tragedies of your
past do not define you, and they do not determine who you
will be in life. You are the arbiter of your own destiny; it is
within your power to determine who you will be in life.

> "Your tragedy
> does not
> determine your
> trajectory!"
> Dr. Cortlan J.
> Wickliff

Furthermore, if you allow it, these challenges can become fuel for your passion.

The next thing to realize is that it is YOUR motivation! The motivation must be personal *to you*. This is not about "knowing your parents' why" or "knowing what your significant other thinks should drive you"—this chapter is not about the motivations of anybody but *you*! It is okay to do things for other people, yes. There is nothing wrong with wearing a specific shirt because your girlfriend wants you to or traveling to a new city because your husband wants you to. However, one of the biggest mistakes we make is going down a difficult path for no other reason than someone else wants us to.

If my only reason for undertaking my 18-year-long educational goals had been because my grandfather wanted one of us to be Dr. Wickliff or because I knew it would have made my dad proud, I might have given up when they passed away. I know this isn't the same for everyone—for some people, the motivation to make a loved one proud grows significantly when they die—but what happens if you grow estranged from the person you started your journey for? Or what happens when the thought of disappointing your family just isn't as scary as it used to be? The harsh reality of relying solely on other people's desires to motivate you is that those motivations can be stolen from you at any time.

> "I do know one thing about me: I don't measure myself by others' expectations or let others define my worth."
> SCJ Sonia Sotomayor

Additionally, you will never be motivated to push past your limits and excel if the source of all of your motivation is the whims and will of other people. If your motivation is not internalized, it is easy to lose sight of it. I am almost certain that your last thought going to sleep and your first thought waking up is not "I hope I make someone else proud" or "I am glad I have gotten one step closer to accomplishing another person's goal." The thing that motivates you through the hard times must be an inescapable and haunting thought. It should be a thought that, if you think about it right before bed, can make you get out of bed to do a bit more work or set your alarm clock for a few minutes earlier.

Put simply, good core motivation that is honest, inspirational, and personal is something that haunts and bullies you into success. Good motivation will force you to stand on your feet when everything else is screaming at you to lie down. Marshall "Eminem" Mathers said it best: "I bully myself 'cause I make me do what I put my mind to…" And that is what finding your personal motivation can do for you.

Now, this is not to say that others cannot motivate you. Even though making my dad proud has been and still is one of my motivations, it isn't the one that drives me the most. If it were, I could have stopped my academic pursuits after my first degree, because my dad would have already been beyond proud of me. You can have as many additional motivations as you want, and some of them may even be core motivators. For example, for parents, one of their core motivators typically is the health and well-being of their children. This motivation is so powerful it makes people accomplish the impossible and soar to unimaginable heights. World heavyweight boxing champion Deontay Wilder's need to pay his daughter's medical bills took him from a novice who had never really boxed before to being an Olympian in three years and the WBC heavyweight champion four years after that. So yes, you can find powerful motivation in other people.

However, it is equally important—if not more so—to find core motivations that can exist independently of everyone else. It is important to identify core motivations that are fully personal, because having all of your core motivators be tethered to someone or something else outside of your control can endanger your continued success. In the case of Wilder, his daughter is healthy and strong now; if he didn't have other things driving him, he would not be able to continue to push forward. People and circumstances come and go, but your drive should stay with you forever.

To that end, I have a challenging but effective exercise for those of you having difficulty finding your motivation(s).

EXERCISE 2: FIND YOUR DRIVE

1. Take a sheet of paper and draw a line down the middle

2. Label one column "Crap" and the other "Cravings."

3. Start with the Cravings side because it tends to be the easier column. Think of the things you most desire but that you don't have or don't have enough of. If money is the first thing that comes to mind, think harder about why you want money. What are the things you most want to buy? Or do you desire to have the power to give orders instead of taking them? What are the reoccurring daydreams that always put a smile on your face? Are there things you lie in bed thinking about? It can be anything, as long as it is H.I.P. (Honest, Inspirational, and Personal). Write them down in your Cravings category. "I want a new house," "I want to marry [person's name]," "I want to be my own boss," "I want this trophy," etc.

4. Now for the Crap. This is difficult. Try to think of the worst experiences or feelings of your life. These would be the handful of times you felt the absolute lowest. It could be an embarrassing experience at work, a family crisis that took a toll on you emotionally, a time when you were made fun of, or any experience you absolutely refuse to ever have again. In the Crap column, write down those feelings and experiences you never want to experience (or never want to experience again). "I never want to be hungry," "I never want to bury a loved one," "I never want to let [person's name] win against me," etc.

5. Somewhere on this page are the motivation(s) that will push you to work harder. Review the list and see which ones resonate with you the most. Ultimately, your core motivation(s) will be the thing on the page that you can't stop thinking about.

6. When you find that core motivation(s), highlight or underline it.

There are two things to note about this exercise. First and foremost, all motivations are not created equal. As I previously stated, I am far more motivated by crap than I am by cravings. The death of my dad has always been a motivating force for me—I never again want to feel the powerlessness and pain I felt that day, the pain of being unable to help or save someone I love. Additionally, I spent a large portion of my life having people underestimating me and writing me off. The feeling of being ignored and marginalized is something I never again want to feel. Essentially, whether it was my tenth-grade English teacher who told me I wouldn't be successful in college writing courses or the pre-law advisor who told me to set my law school sights lower, I became highly driven to prove people wrong when they said I couldn't or wouldn't succeed. Consequently, I made an A in every college writing/English course I took and attended a top-three ranked law school.

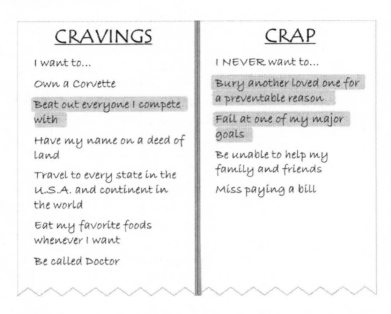

CRAVINGS	CRAP
I want to...	I NEVER want to...
Own a Corvette	Bury another loved one for a preventable reason
Beat out everyone I compete with	Fail at one of my major goals
Have my name on a deed of land	Be unable to help my family and friends
Travel to every state in the U.S.A. and continent in the world	Miss paying a bill
Eat my favorite foods whenever I want	
Be called Doctor	

Secondly, know that your motivations will change over time, so update them occasionally. While I am motivated by crap more than cravings, even from a young age, I loved (and I still do love) gumbo and snow crabs; this is an example of one of my cravings. If I could, I would have had those dishes all of the time. So, throughout elementary, middle school, and high school, I worked hard to one day be able to afford to have gumbo and snow crabs whenever I wanted. Then, when I went off to college, I was exposed to the world of well-prepared steaks. Now, I get just as much motivation out of an excellent filet as I do a cluster of snow crabs. In other words, my cravings have changed.

One aspect of pursuing goals in order to satiate your cravings is that you are going to eventually get what you crave. This is another reason why your motivations will periodically update themselves. Let's say you were motivated to work hard so that you could get married and have a family. When you work hard and achieve the goals that allow you to have a family, then getting a family won't be motivation anymore—you will need to find a new motivator.

> "Each of you, as individuals, must pick your own goals. Listen to others, but do not become a blind follower."
> SCJ. Thurgood Marshall

Perhaps that new motivation will be having the ability to take care of your family or being a good role model for your kids. Similarly, if one of your motivations for working hard to be the number-one salesperson at your company was to be able to afford to buy a house, you will need to replace that craving with a new motivation after you get your house. Make sure to periodically revisit this exercise at various stages of your life.

Once you have picked motivations that truly resonate with you, make sure to keep them in the forefront of your mind. My greatest motivator is working towards having the ability to take care of the people I love. Whenever I am about to go on a big interview, give a major speech, or work on a critical project, I keep reminders of that motivation around me. For me, those reminders come in the form of something from Texas. Although I have family in major cities and small towns around the world, our family hometowns are in Liberty County: Ames, Liberty, and Raywood, three adjoining towns in East Texas. For this reason, I generally wear something that reminds me of Texas. These reminders include wearing things like my Texas flag cufflinks, cowboy belts, and memorabilia from my Texas schools. Whenever I wear one of these items, I am reminded of all the people back home whom I am working hard to protect.

If you do not have a simple portable memento that can remind you of your motivations, here is another exercise I used when I first left for college.

EXERCISE 3: DRIVEN MEMENTOES

1. Identify the areas where you spend the most time, especially the area where you spend the most time working. In college, I spent the most time at my desk and in my car.

2. Identify the items that you spend the most time with. For me, those items were my three-ring binder and my laptop.

3. Place reminders of your motivations wherever you spend the most time and on whatever item or device you spend the most time with. You could place a vision board in one of these locations as well. For me, I had a board of pictures of all my family and friends on the wall in front of my desk, a cross hanging in my car on the rearview mirror, a collage of famous people I was competing with on my three-ring binder, and a picture of a new Corvette on my laptop wallpaper. Each of those things reminded me of something that motivated me.

Why is choosing a memento important? "The squeaky wheel gets the oil," "the nail that sticks out is most likely to get hammered," etc. So many sayings essentially tell us that the thing that is the most obvious or annoying gets addressed first. It is easy to forget about an abstract concept or an old promise that motivates you, but it becomes a lot harder to forget when a constant reminder of it is staring you in the face on a daily basis.

The point of this exercise is to give you constant reminders of your motivations. These mementos will keep you focused on why you do the things you do. When you embark upon your journey towards making your dreams a reality, you need to constantly remind yourself of why you are driven to achieve those dreams. When you lose sight of your core motivation(s), it can be easy to forget why you are working so hard, and that makes it easier to quit.

Quitting cannot be an option. By keeping constant reminders of your motivators around you, you make the discomfort of quitting exceed the difficulty of finishing. Understand that working towards your goals is going to get hard—worthwhile accomplishments do not come easily! For me, every time I saw a picture of a Corvette, I remembered my dad looking back at me. I thought about the people he couldn't be around to take care of, and I felt that it was my responsibility to do so in his place. I remembered my mom, my brothers, my grandparents, and all of the other people who relied on me or one day might rely on me. With their images in my head, how could I quit? How could I fail to become the man Dad expected me to be? By looking at those mementos, I was reminded of my core motivations (e.g., never fail at one of my major goals, never bury another loved one for a preventable reason, etc.), and I could work harder and longer as a result.

The effect of your memento(s) is to make sure you never forget your motivations. If you chose one that truly resonates with you, it can be a powerful tool in your quest to achieve your goals. An effective reminder of your core motivations will push you to do more than you might think possible and will allow you to push the limits of your capability.

Chapter 4:
Establish Goals

     Goals are the framework upon which accomplishments are built. Whether it is a towering skyscraper, sprawling bridge, or simple home, every enduring structure starts off as a frame. So too should your accomplishments be framed or outlined before you start to work towards them.

     How do you establish your framework? Every goal or set of goals starts as a dream. A lot of people use the words "dreams" and "goals" as if they are interchangeable, but they are not. What is the difference between a dream and a goal? There are numerous schools of thought about this subject. I ascribe to the belief that dreams are destinations and goals are the bricks that pave your path to your dream.

Look at Dr. King's "I Have a Dream" speech. This is one of the—if not *the*—most well-known examples of an articulated dream. In this speech, Dr. King shares his dream for a desegregated world where equality abounds. This was a dream he had established before he made this speech and one that was shared by many of his contemporary peers. However, simply dreaming it was not enough. No matter how widespread or strong a dream is, a dream that is never paired with goals is never reached. To get closer to that dream of equality, Dr. King and his contemporary peers established concrete goals, such as the end of Jim Crow laws, the protection of voters' rights, the desegregation of public institutions, etc. It was the pursuit of these concrete goals that has gotten us closer to Dr. King's dream; however, all great achievements start with a dream. Thus, *your* extraordinary accomplishments should likewise begin now with a dream.

> "Be strong-minded and always think that the impossible is possible."
> Selena Quintanilla–Pérez

The most important thing to remember is that no dream is too outlandish; anything is possible if you are willing to proactively work towards it. Often, people do not pursue dreams because they do not believe they have the ability to achieve them. Do not forget the groundwork of belief we established in the previous chapters!

If you are having trouble identifying a dream to pursue, think back to the previous chapter. At this point in your journey through this book, you should know the things that motivate you. Think about what you want from life. What are your strongest motivators? If, as in the previous chapter, you treat the pursuit of your dreams like a relationship, what do you need and desire from that relationship?

Once you have a clear picture of what you want from life and what you desire from your accomplishments, do some research. Figure out what types of dreams and goals fulfill your desires. What are the types of dreams that, if you pursue them and achieve them, would allow you to avoid all of the crap you want to avoid and fulfill all of the cravings you have? When you start doing that research, you will see a lot of potential options open up to you. Some of these paths will be more difficult and/or rewarding than others.

Think carefully about which pathways actually appeal to you. Is there something you have fantasized about? Is there someone you admire whom you want to emulate? Or is there something you have always wanted to do that can also satiate your motivations? When you start thinking about and answering these questions, you will find yourself naturally gravitating towards a handful of ideas.

There are no limitations when it comes to setting your dream, and there is only one rule: *Aim as high as you can!* You should believe in yourself enough to pursue any dream you can dare to dream, no matter how ambitious, bold, or awe-inspiring it is.

Think about the times you have fantasized about all of the fantastic things you want from life. Think of all the wonderful things you lie awake imagining and daydreaming about. Your dream can be anything: playing in the majors, owning a business, or being a surgeon, world-famous artist, famous actor/actress, fighter pilot, or even a racecar driver. At this stage of your journey, you don't have to be overly specific—that comes in later chapters. You can dream any dream in the world, and when you find one you want to come true, the next step is to turn that dream into an emphatic statement.

I have a simple exercise for you. It's a slight variation of a leadership exercise my mom showed me, and it is an exercise I have done at schools, universities, conferences, and companies around the country.

EXERCISE 4: VISIONARY VOCALS

1. Find an area where you are alone or do not mind shouting.
2. Pick a dream you want to achieve.
3. Write it down. But, instead of writing your dream as a desire (e.g., "I want to grow my department" or "I want to be the top salesman in my region"), you are going to write down your dream as if it has already occurred. Examples: "<u>I am</u> the newest manager at my company," "<u>I am</u> a successful business owner," "<u>I am</u> the best salesman in my region."
4. Read this statement to yourself a few times.
5. Then, when you are ready, state it loudly and proudly.
6. State it again, even louder.
7. Repeat Step 6 five more times.

In corporate America, they call this establishing a "vision" or a "vision statement." This is essentially what your Chief Executive Officer (CEO) is doing at your annual company meeting—loudly and clearly articulating a vision for the company. In Southern Baptist churches, they call this "Naming and Claiming It." The premise behind the practice is that you will never achieve a dream if you aren't able to very vocally proclaim it.

There are two reasons for this. First, words have power, and we oftentimes underestimate how much they can influence our subconscious. If I tell you, "Don't think about a purple elephant. Under no circumstances should the image of a purple elephant cross your mind at this exact moment. Whatever you do, don't think of a big PURPLE ELEPHANT!"

What are you likely to have just thought about? The vast majority of the people reading this sentence will have visualized some form of a purple elephant. You are able to visualize this even if you have never seen an elephant that was purple. Why?

> "I am the greatest, I said that even before I knew I was."
> Muhammad Ali

Words—whether you say them, read them, or hear them—can force your mind to create mental images. This is the power of words, and you can use it for your benefit. If you proudly proclaim, "I am a surgeon!" then you are going to vividly imagine yourself in scrubs standing in an operating room. It will be in that moment that the idea of fulfilling your dream doesn't seem as farfetched as it had in the past. This makes you more likely to actually make that mental image a reality.

This is why, in general, you have to be careful about what you watch, say, and listen to. The power of words can also work against you if you are bombarding your mind with negative imagery or counterproductive ideas. This is also why it is so important to engage in the affirmations we discussed in the "Believe" chapter. It is equally important that you don't speak negatively about yourself or verbally undermine your confidence. Remember, words lead to visualization, visualization leads to action, and action leads to achievement. Whether that achievement is positive or negative often depends on the words you let enter your psyche.

The first reason for the preceding exercise was to get your mind to visualize; the second reason was to make sure your mind doesn't forget. I have found that it is easy to forget a dream, but it is much harder to forget the time you shouted, "I am a successful business owner!" seven times. And the louder you can proclaim your dream as a reality, the more you will believe it. If you are going to accomplish something spectacular, you cannot lose sight of or doubt your ability to reach the destination. Like Peter walking on water, the moment you start to doubt, you will falter (Matt. 14:22-33). So use this exercise to fix your focus on your goals.

Like companies who print posters of their vision statements and place them all over the office, place reminders of your proclamations around you. This can be anything from mementos you carry with you to remind you of your commitments to sticky-note reminders you strategically place around your home and workspace. You should also periodically repeat the above exercise if ever you start to feel uncertain about your trajectory.

At this point, your dream is well-established, you have emphatically stated it, and you have started to believe that it is possible. The next step is to turn your dream into goals. Your dream is a destination, and your goals are the stepping stones that will get you to that destination. Now that you know where you are and where you want to be, it is time to fill in the middle.

> "The path from dreams to success does exist. May you have the vision to find it, the courage to get on to it, and the perseverance to follow it."
> Dr. Kalpana Chawla

In order to do this, you must decide the three to six major milestones you must achieve to make your dream come true. Let's look at my educational dream to become "Dr. Wickliff." In order to accomplish that dream, I knew I needed a medical degree or a PhD; thus, getting a PhD became one of my goals. In order to get a PhD, you must already have two other degrees, so I picked two degrees that I wanted to attain prior to starting my PhD. The three major goals that would lead me to my dream were set. My goals were to get a BS in engineering, a JD, and a PhD, which would allow me to make my dream of being Dr. Wickliff come true.

Consider the example of someone who dreams of becoming a professional musician. How might that translate into concrete goals? They could set a goal to learn how to read and write music. Other goals could include scoring an album, saving the money needed to pay for studio time to record an album, and getting singles played on certain radio stations. With each goal they accomplish, they get closer and closer to their dream.

In establishing your goals, there are really only three rules. The first rule is that you can't achieve big dreams without big milestone goals. Using our building analogy, all structures are limited by the scope of their frame. An 80-story building has an 80-story frame. If your goals are the frame that you build your dreams upon, do not expect to be able to achieve big dreams in life if your goals are small. In other words, do not expect that achieving ordinary goals will lead you to an extraordinary dream.

My academic dream would not have been possible if I had not set aggressive interim academic goals. Similarly, if your dream is to be a Country Music Association award-winning artist, your goals must be just as ambitious as that dream. Your milestone goals shouldn't be just to make an album or play a concert—your major milestones should be the kind of goals that directly lead to your dream. Recording an album and playing at a concert are not ambitious enough goals to lead to the dream of winning a CMA award. If winning that award is your dream, your goals should include ambitious achievements like making a platinum-selling album or going on tour with one of the previous "Entertainer of the Year" award winners. Remember, ambitious accomplishments are necessary to achieve ambitious dreams.

The second rule is that your goals must be grounded in your motivation. Think about any sturdy structure you have seen. Whenever you see a large skyscraper being built, the metal beams that comprise its framework are actually embedded into the concrete of its foundation. So too should your goals be grounded deeply in your strongest motivations. You must be able to clearly articulate why you are pursuing a goal and why that goal is meaningful to you. If you cannot, then your goals can be easily torn down.

When you are working towards exceptional achievements, you are going to want to give up at some point—I cannot tell you how many times I contemplated quitting. The ultimate determinant of your long-term success will be whether you are on a path where the pain of failure exceeds the discomfort of continued effort. If you are

> "Push through the pain—giving up hurts more."
> Vegeta
> *(Dragon Ball Z)*

pursuing a goal or a dream that you don't have a strong reason for wanting, you will give up when things become difficult. The best way to combat this phenomenon is to make sure that you are highly motivated to achieve each of your goals.

My core motivations center on being able to prove what I am capable of and to take care of what I love. Every dream I have had and every goal I have set are well-grounded in both of those motivations. For example, the reason I went for a BS in engineering rather than one of the more traditional and shorter pre-law degrees is because I knew engineers make good salaries, and good salaries allow you to take care of people. Knowing what I had already lost for lack of money and what an engineering degree could keep me from losing in the future made the idea of *not* achieving my goal repugnant and unthinkable. That is what having a strong motivation to achieve your goals can do for you. So make sure that any goal you set is well-grounded in a strong motivation.

The last rule of identifying your goals is that for every one dream, you should have multiple goals. A lot of financial advisors strongly recommend that when you are paying off debts, you start by paying off your smaller debts first and then work your way up to your larger debts. Why? If you are paying off all of your debt anyway, it really doesn't matter the order, right? The reason for this recommendation is that they want you to build momentum with early successes and see progress. Studies of human behavior show that without those intermediate milestone accomplishments, people are more likely to give up.

It doesn't take a medical degree to know why people give up more easily without intermediate achievements—there are few things more frustrating than working really hard for a long period of time and having no tangible results or accomplishments to show for it. If after a few months of doing something, you still see little to no progress, you are going to start believing that it is pointless, and you will give up. The same principle applies to pursuing your dream. You need to break your dream into reasonable and digestible portions so that you can see progress over time.

In general, if you fail to establish intermediate goals between you and your dream, accomplishing your dream will begin to feel overwhelming and daunting. Take, for example, my dream to become Dr. Wickliff. My dream was not just to become Cortlan the engineer or even Attorney Wickliff. However, giving myself major milestones allowed me to feel like I was making progress. I spent eleven years in college. Without those intermediary milestones, there would have been no way for me to gauge my success or benchmark my progress. It would have been difficult to maintain my motivation to finish the last year of my journey if I hadn't accomplished anything tangible for the first ten years! For this reason, I encourage you to think carefully about how you can divide your dream into multiple goals. This step is especially crucial if you have a dream that will take years or even decades to accomplish.

Also, we are going to talk later about celebrating your victories. One of the greatest ways to keep yourself motivated is to be able to celebrate major milestones along the way to achieving your great accomplishments. However, in order to be able to celebrate these victories, you must have milestones to mark your progress.

Other than these three rules—*set big goals*, *ground your goals in your motivations*, and *have multiple (at least three to six) goals per dream*—you have the latitude to set whatever goals you think you can build upon to achieve your dream.

Once you have selected your three to six major goals, you must refine them to make sure they are well-defined goals. An exercise that helps with this process is called setting S.M.A.R.T. Goals. You may have seen some variation of this exercise before. The premise is that every goal you set should be a S.M.A.R.T. Goal: a goal that is *Specific, Measurable, Attainable, Relevant,* and *Timely.* So for each goal you set or think about setting for yourself, try this exercise.

EXERCISE 5: DEVELOP S.M.A.R.T. GOALS

1. Take a sheet of paper and divide it into five rows.

2. In the first row, write the word "Specific"; in the second, the word "Measurable"; in the third, the word "Attainable"; in the fourth, the word "Relevant"; and in the last, the word "Timely."

SPECIFIC	I will lose 30 pounds
MEASURABLE	I will measure success at the end by whether or not I weigh 30lbs less than when I started.
ATTAINABLE	YES!
RELEVANT	Reduces my risk of distracting health problems and gives me more energy to dedicate to working towards my goals
TIMELY	I will give myself ninety days to achieve this goal.

3. In the first row (i.e., Specific), write out your goal with specificity. This means that you shouldn't write ambiguous or imprecise statements. For example, "Getting healthier" or "Exercising more" is not a specific goal. There isn't a clear way to determine the steps you need to take to achieve any of these goals. If you want to get healthier, a specific goal could be "Lower my blood pressure to less than 120/80." Or instead of "Exercising more," a specific goal could be "Lose 30 lbs. and drop X number of pant/dress sizes." Both of those statements establish a goal that is clear enough for you to understand what specifically you need to be working towards. This allows you to create a concrete plan for achieving the goal. When I was first going through this exercise, I listed the specific goals of *graduating with an engineering degree, graduating with a law degree,* and *graduating with a PhD.* Even in my professional career, I have been able to use this exercise: I have had specific goals like "Increase my company's profit by 20%" and "Be hired in a senior management position making a minimum of X dollars."

4. In the second row (i.e., Measurable), explain how you are going to measure success. This means that generic phrases like "get better at," "do more of," or "improve" should not appear in your goal statement. By listing the specific goal of losing 30 pounds and/or dropping a specific number of pant/dress sizes, there are clear methods you can use to determine progress towards success and when success is achieved. In the case of my academic goal, I could measure success in the form of three diplomas. I knew I had succeeded when I had received a diploma for each degree, and I could measure progress in credit hours towards each degree. Similarly, a 20% increase in profits is

something I could measure easily with dollars. Make sure that all of your goals have a tangible method of measuring progress and success that can be captured in this row.

5. Skip the third row for now. For the fourth row (i.e., Relevant), ask yourself, "Is this goal relevant?" If it is, write out how the goal is relevant. What does this mean? We have talked extensively about making sure that your goals are grounded in your motivations— well, this question is asking you how this goal is going to help you satisfy one or more of your motivations. The purpose of this step is to make sure that you are not going to work haphazardly towards your goals. This step reminds you of why you are going to work so hard to achieve this goal! If you cannot explain the relevance of your goal in terms of one or more of your core motivations, then choose a different goal.

For me, several reasons made my academic goals relevant. First and foremost, many people had told me that I couldn't accomplish these goals, and that only motivated me to want to prove them wrong. As we previously discussed, a motivator can change and/or disappear altogether, so it helps if a goal is grounded in multiple motivators. I also knew that my academic journey would allow me to get a great job and would grant me access to opportunities I could use to take care of my friends, family, and anyone I care about. Additionally, the salary for those jobs would allow me to buy all the snow crabs and steak I wanted. For these reasons, I could say that each academic goal was relevant to me. This row is the time to make sure that every major goal you pick is grounded in your core motivations. Remember, it helps if they are grounded in multiple motivators.

6. In the last row, give yourself a deadline for achieving your goals. This is important, because if you give yourself infinite time to do something, you are in jeopardy of failing to accomplish your goals. If I had said "Graduate with a BS, JD, and PhD" without giving myself a timetable, I could have postponed starting my journey indefinitely.

When setting a timetable, be aggressive. Unreasonably long timetables don't require as much effort and can make an ambitious goal merely average. When one of my goals was to increase my company profits by 20%, I set a timetable of one year for that goal. That timetable made that goal ambitious. If I had given myself infinite time, I could have put in no effort and waited a decade or two for inflation to drive up revenue.

Remember, ambitious dreams require ambitious goals. Set timetables that push your capabilities! It is okay if it ends up taking a little longer than you would like. Setting an aggressive schedule will make you work more consistently and proactively towards your goals.

I also recommend setting a timetable that is earlier than is actually necessary. For me, I absolutely wanted to finish all three degrees before my 26th birthday, so I made my timetable such that I would finish my last degree a year prior, when I was still 24 years old. The reason for this recommendation is that setbacks are inevitable, and it is helpful to give yourself a little cushion. Ultimately, my timetable took a full year longer than expected, and had it not been for my pursuit of an aggressive timetable, I would not have accomplished my goal graduating with my PhD before my 26th birthday.

7. Now, return to the third row. Is your goal attainable? This section is personal to you. What I mean is that you have to believe that you can achieve this goal. It doesn't matter what anybody else thinks—all that matters is that *you* believe it is possible. If you don't believe you can do what you have written down, edit it until you do. I emphasize the personal nature of this question because if you pick a lofty goal, a lot of people (including family members and friends) may tell you it is not possible. I cannot count the number of times somebody explained to me why some of my personal, professional, or academic goals were unrealistic or impossible. However, *I* believed that they were attainable, and that was all that mattered. Similarly, when answering the question of whether your goal is attainable, your opinion is the only one that matters.

If you cannot complete this exercise for a goal, then it is likely a goal that is too ill-defined and ambiguous to pursue. When a goal is not *Specific, Measurable, Attainable, Relevant,* or *Timely*, it is hard to define when success is achieved and even harder to understand your relative progress. As previously stated, not knowing how close you are to success and not being able to determine how much progress you have made can make it hard to maintain your determination. Furthermore, when you believe that a goal is unattainable, you will lack the will to earnestly pursue that goal. Pursuing goals that are not S.M.A.R.T. Goals can be frustrating, and the experience increases the likelihood that you will quit before accomplishing your dream.

Therefore, if you are unable to complete this exercise with a particular goal, refine the goal more before you attempt to develop a plan to achieve it. In some cases, this will require you to completely reevaluate your goals; in others, it will just require a little tweaking. Regardless, do not actively pursue any goals that are not S.M.A.R.T. (*Specific*, *Measurable*, *Attainable*, *Relevant* and *Timely*) Goals.

> "Real change, enduring change, happens one step at a time."
> SCJ Ruth Bader Ginsburg

Chapter 5:
Create a Plan

When you are laying the framework for your accomplishments, you will set major milestone goals that will be measured in months or years. That is the framework we established in the previous chapter. Yet, in order to achieve major milestone goals that are long-term, you are going to have to achieve shorter-term goals along the way. The next step in your personal construction project is to create your detailed blueprint of those short-term goals. The aim of this chapter is for you to identify the steps necessary to achieve your major milestone accomplishments and your dream.

In this chapter, you will learn methods for creating a thorough plan to achieve your dream. You may ask, "Why is this necessary? I already know what I need to do." But knowing where you want to end up is not the same thing as knowing exactly how to get there. Most major milestones require dozens if not hundreds of intermediary steps to achieve them. These steps not only include big steps like graduations, job interviews, and project submissions, they also include smaller, more easily overlooked steps, like consent forms, preliminary submission deadlines, and required signatures. If you don't take the time to identify all of those intermediate steps, you will likely miss some of them. Those kinds of lapses can be costly.

> "... tomorrow belongs to those who prepare for it today."
> Malcolm X

The world is full of unforgiving bureaucracy, and not everyone will make an exception. There are people who have lost millions of dollars because they forgot a submission deadline. I also personally know people who delayed their graduation by a year or more just because they failed to turn in a one-page form on time. Don't derail your journey because you overlooked a little rule or requirement!

Additionally, if the planning process is done properly, it will allow you to identify potential stumbling blocks before you encounter them. This gives you an opportunity to plan for difficult circumstances before they occur.

Successful people plan for the famine during the feast. Some segments of your journey will be easier than others and will offer you more access to resources and people than during other times. You want to optimize those good/easy times by preparing for what you will need in the more difficult segments of your journey. If you wait until the hard times to start figuring out how you will handle those hard times, you will have waited too long and will have likely missed some opportunities.

For example, the best time to start planning and working towards starting a company is not when you are already out of work or already done with school. Although you can still be successful regardless of when you make the leap, your journey will be far more difficult if you wait until your safety net is gone before starting the planning process. While you are in a university setting, you have access to people and resources that you will never have access to again—think of the centers, laboratories, facilities, subject matter experts, instructors, printing (poster, 3D, circuit board, etc.), and computing centers on campus, and the inexpensive software available for purchase or use. Similarly, when you are employed, you have access to people and resources you will not have access to again; additionally, your abilities to purchase equipment, attend conferences, and secure resources are higher when you have a steady income.

You want to be able to maximize these situations and work towards what's next. Whether it is something as basic as working on a business plan or starting to study for an entrance exam well in advance or something as big as finding a sponsor to invest in the next stages of your journey, you want to be proactively preparing yourself for the next phase at all times. The only way you will be able to do that is if you know what your next steps are. Thus, planning increases the likelihood that you will successfully identify and navigate through tough situations and avoid pitfalls.

The technique I recommend for creating your plan is to plan both forward and backwards. What does that mean? A forward plan is where you make a list of the tasks and steps you must complete to meet your major milestone goals. Let us use the example of taking a road trip from downtown Austin, TX to Houston, TX. If you were planning forward, you would start from downtown Austin and plan the roads and highways you need to take to get to Houston. One of the shortest and most straightforward routes is to take Interstate 35 to Hwy 290 East, which dead-ends in Houston. This is the likely route people (and most GPS systems) would pick to get to Houston from Austin.

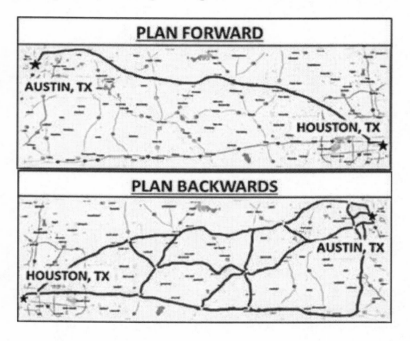

Planning backwards is when you start with the goal and plan from the goal to your starting position. Your plan starts with the step that must immediately precede the accomplishment, then the step that must precede that step, and so on until you get to your starting position. Going back to our road trip example, if you were planning backwards, you would start from Houston. The first step would be to ask which highways go in the direction of Austin. You will find that Interstate 10 as well as Highway 290 are potential routes towards Austin. Once on those two highways, there are multiple routes to get to Austin. You would trace each of those routes backwards and see all of the different ways they could get you to Austin. In this context, planning backwards generates more than a half-dozen different routes.

> "If you fail to plan, you plan to fail!"

Individually, planning forward and planning backwards can be useful tools for creating a plan. However, depending on how you think, using one method without the other can lead to less-thorough planning. The reason for planning both forward and backwards is that it forces you to consider alternate possible pathways to your goal. By approaching the problem from different vantage points, you can force yourself to think outside the box. In the previous example, forward planning only yielded one route, whereas approaching the problem from the backwards perspective gave us multiple, more detailed route options. Sometimes the opposite is true and forward planning is the method that allows you to generate multiple possible detailed approaches.

Several cognitive biases (i.e., shortcut mental connections/assumptions you make to speed up decision-making) exist that cause you to assume that your pathways are more limited. The goal is to force you to approach achieving each intermediate goal, major goal, and dream from at least two vantage points. When done properly, that can combat some of the preexisting cognitive biases that could otherwise prevent you from making the best-informed decisions during your planning process. Thus, using both methods simultaneously is a powerful tool for creating plans to achieve long-term goals.

Consider the real-world example of my wanting to become Dr. Wickliff and work in a technical field. When I planned forward, I thought I had to get a bachelor's degree and then go to medical school and then complete a residency, at which point the goal I established while still in elementary school would have been accomplished. But medical doctors are not the only people with the title of Doctor. So when I started from the goal and worked backwards, I realized that I could get a medical degree, a pharmaceutical doctorate, a doctorate in veterinary medicine, or a PhD in any number of disciplines, including in science, technology, and engineering fields. The first step in this backwards planning opened up several options that I might not otherwise have known existed.

Now, I want you to do an exercise in planning forward and backwards. The more thoroughly you do your backwards and forward planning, the more options you will give yourself in accomplishing your goals and the clearer your action items will become. If done properly, this exercise might cause you to change some of the major milestones that you established in the previous section. That is okay! The most important thing is to make sure that any goal you set—whether it's big or small, major or intermediary—is a S.M.A.R.T. Goal that gets you closer to your dream.

EXERCISE 6: PLAN FORWARD AND BACKWARDS

1. Start by planning forward.

2. This may end up taking more space than one sheet of paper, but for now, let's start with one sheet of paper.

3. Write on the top-left corner the word "now."

4. On the bottom-right corner, write whatever your big dream is.

5. In between the two points, I want you to write down the three to six major milestones that made up your framework from the previous chapter. Do your best to space them out evenly.

6. In between "now" and the first milestone, write out three major steps that must occur before you can reach the first milestone. Do your best to space them out evenly.

7. Repeat Step 6 between each of the major milestones until you get to the final accomplished dream. If you have already identified multiple possible pathways to your dream, write them down as well. If you run out of space, do this on another sheet of paper.

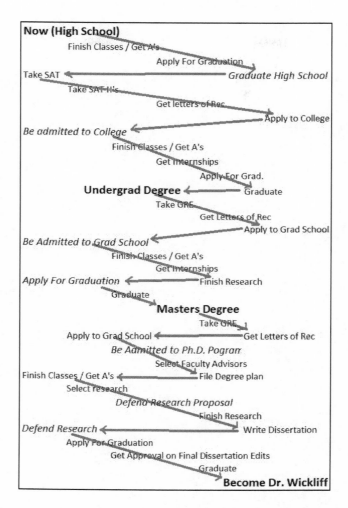

Now (High School)
Finish Classes / Get A's
Apply For Graduation
Take SAT ← Graduate High School
Take SAT II's
Get letters of Rec
Apply to College
Be admitted to College ←
Finish Classes / Get A's
Get Internships
Apply For Grad.
Undergrad Degree ← Graduate
Take GRE
Get Letters of Rec
Apply to Grad School
Be Admitted to Grad School ←
Finish Classes / Get A's
Get Internships
Apply For Graduation ← Finish Research
Graduate
Masters Degree
Take GRE
Apply to Grad School ← Get Letters of Rec
Be Admitted to Ph.D. Pogram
Select Faculty Advisors
Finish Classes / Get A's ← File Degree plan
Select research
Defend Research Proposal
Finish Research
Defend Research ← Write Dissertation
Apply For Graduation
Get Approval on Final Dissertation Edits
Graduate
Become Dr. Wickliff

8. Now plan backwards. This tends to be less linear because you will find pathways you didn't know existed.

9. Get another sheet of paper.

10. Write on the top-left corner the word "now."

11. On the bottom-right corner, write whatever your big dream is.

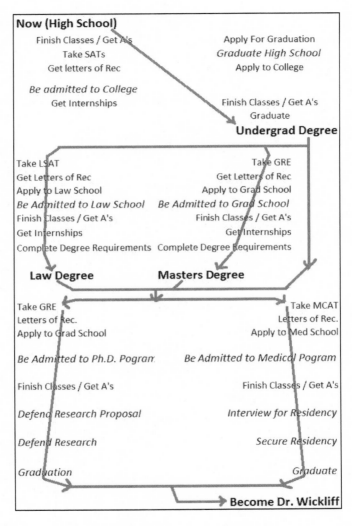

12. Starting from the dream, list the steps that precede or could precede the accomplishment of your dream.

13. Then list the steps that precede or could precede the steps listed.

14. Repeat this process until you work your way back up to "now."

15. Any time one of your pathways leads back to one of your previously selected major milestones, circle them.

16. Compare the backwards and forward planning. Are there any pathways that do not include your previously selected milestones? Consider whether there are other major milestones you should pursue. Typically, the first time you do forward and backwards planning for a goal, the papers do not look the same. If they are identical in the first iteration, do some research to see if you are missing any steps or possible alternative pathways.

17. Are there major steps or other goals that are included in multiple pathways? If you have multiple possible pathways, you can choose to get to the same destination; identifying steps that are on multiple pathways can afford you more options as you progress through your journey.

An example of this process could be an accountant who has the dream of starting a business. The accountant is uncertain whether they want to start a general store, a delivery company, or a property management company. The accountant decides that one of the prerequisite steps to starting a business is to get more work experience. To get this work experience, the accountant can choose to either work at a property management company or work at a venture capital firm. Which job should the accountant take?

If the accountant works for a property management company as an accountant, the experience may not be transferrable to other businesses. But if the accountant works with a venture capital firm, the experience of raising money will be transferable to any business. Thus, the accountant should strongly consider working at the more generally applicable position (i.e., the venture capital firm). Choose pathways that allow you the most opportunities to achieve your dreams.

18. What are the steps that both the forward and backwards plans have in common? These steps will likely be non-optional steps.

19. Throughout this process, you will gather more information about steps and pathways you didn't know existed. Consider repeating this process once or twice to refine your forward and backwards plan.

20. Based on the final backwards and forward pathways, select a combined plan which includes "now," three to six major milestones, your dream, and at least three to five intermediate steps between each one of them. This is your blueprint.

Doing this process in an electronic spreadsheet or in some other computer program may prove to be easier, especially if your goals are intricate or you are still figuring out what steps each goal entails. An electronic version will also allow you to easily edit and expand your goals and the intermediate steps.

Even when you finish this process, you are not finished with your plan—the plan you have generated in this chapter is only a starting point. Your plan is a "living document," meaning that, like all living things, it should *consume*, *grow*, and *adapt*.

> "A person has to remember that the road to success is always under construction... it is not easy becoming successful."
> Steve Harvey

What does a plan consume? Information! As you progress through your journey, you are going to learn more about the steps you will need to take to achieve your goals. Whether you get the information as part of a formal document, find it while looking online, or get it from a conversation with a trusted resource, whenever you gain more information on how to accomplish a major milestone goal or intermediary step, that information should be incorporated into your plan.

The first day I began each of my degrees, I was given a degree plan and/or graduation requirements. These were checklists that contained every step I needed to complete in order to graduate. Similarly, whenever I would start a new job or new project at work, I would be given expectations and project goals. Whether formally written or given in an informal conversation, this information provided me with an understanding of what I needed to be successful on the job. Every deadline, action item, checklist, syllabus, to-do list, development plan, and the like that you receive on your journey becomes additional information that you need to feed into your plan.

The incorporation of new information into your plan means it is going to get bigger. Your plan *should* grow over time! It doesn't have to all be captured on one sheet of paper or in one Excel file; in fact, if done properly, the plan shouldn't fit on one page. As you expand your plan, you will likely engage in forward and backwards planning for several of your intermediate steps and milestone goals. Thus, you will have several checklists, flowcharts, and diagrams that constitute your total plan. This is a good thing! Just make sure to never lose sight of your overall dream while pursuing a major milestone goal, and don't lose sight of your milestone goals while completing intermediate steps.

The last way in which your plan will resemble a living organism is that it should adapt to changing circumstances. As will be discussed in later chapters, you will come across unforeseen situations that make your plan infeasible, impractical, or inefficient. In those circumstances, failing to change your plan could result in failing to accomplish your dream. Do not be so fixated on adhering to the plan that you miss opportunities to achieve your goals and dreams. You cannot be expected to account for everything that might happen a year from now, let alone five or ten years from now. As you get new information and circumstances change, adapt!

> "Be bold in your caring, be bold
> in your dreaming and above all
> else, always do your best."
> Pres. George Bush, Sr.

Chapter 6:
Start Building!

A completed work is far more impressive than a planned masterpiece. Oftentimes, we let the quest for "great" be the enemy of achieving "good" and get stuck in a pattern of analysis paralysis. Analysis paralysis occurs when you overanalyze a decision or action to the point that you never actually make a choice and end up in a paralyzed or inactive state. Essentially, we often continue to outline and plan and revise and amend…and basically do everything BUT act.

I have observed four main reasons why people end up in a state of analysis paralysis: 1. *Can't Find a Dream*, 2. *Chasing the Perfect Plan,* 3. *Fear of Failure,* and 4. *Fear of Success.*

When initially writing this chapter, I had failed to consider one important reason why people have trouble starting to build towards their dream, namely that some people have trouble figuring out *what* dream they want to pursue. In the years since publishing the first edition of this book, I have gotten to tour around the country speaking with students and professionals of all ages. Something that I heard on several occasions was that people were having trouble identifying a dream to pursue.

I want to emphasize that this is perfectly normal and acceptable; however, it is *not* acceptable to use that uncertainty as an excuse to be stagnant. If you cannot identify a big dream to chase, then identify some small goals to pursue. This could be any type of goal that will help you be better positioned to achieve a dream when you do develop one. Examples include different types of monetary, health, academic, and professional S.M.A.R.T. Goals: *save a certain amount of money, lose a certain amount of weight, become fluent in popular business languages (e.g., Chinese, Japanese, Spanish), get promoted to vice president of a company, lower blood pressure to a particular level, get a particular credit score, and/or attain a particular degree (preferably one that has relevance to a wide variety of industries and occupations).* All of these types of goals position you to be better prepared for any occupation, career, or aspiration.

Some people might retort with, "But I don't want to waste time."

If you are sitting around waiting to figure out your dream before you start working on it, then *that* is wasting time. It's similar to meeting somebody for dinner when you haven't picked a restaurant. You can waste time by sitting around, or you can do something—you may not know exactly where you want to go, but you know the place won't be in your living room and you won't go there in your pajamas. So it is an efficient use of time to start preparing to leave the house even if you end up needing to change your shirt, and it is wise to start driving out of your neighborhood even if you end up subtly changing directions. In the same manner, it is never a waste of time to progress towards being better positioned to achieve a dream even when you have not developed a dream to pursue. In my experience, every dream can be aided by acquiring new skill sets, assets, and/or knowledge, even if the only benefit is making you more well-rounded and relatable.

Increasing your relatability is a great networking tool. We are going to discuss networking in more detail in the "Get the Right Team" chapter, but basically, any commonality you share with a potential employer, coach, mentor, or sponsor makes it more likely they will want to work with you. Something as simple as a shared hobby, knowledge of an obscure reference, a mutual interest, or a common travel experience can lay the groundwork for a great working relationship. Thus, the more skill sets, knowledge, and general experiences you acquire, the more you increase your overall relatability.

> "If you can't figure out your purpose, figure out your passion"
> Bp. T.D. Jakes

You can use a thought exercise to help you identify some potential dreams or goals to pursue, which involves self-examination.

EXERCISE 7: FIND YOUR DREAM

1. Identify and make a list of ALL of the things you are exceptionally good at and/or ALL of the ways in which you are naturally gifted. I emphasize "all" because I don't care how random or seemingly

useless the talent/gift is, it should still make the list.

2. Looking at that list, check off everything that brings you joy or that you find yourself often doing for free.

3. Take that list and research how people have monetized that skill set and/or think of creative ways *you* can turn that skill set into a business/occupation.

4. Based on the descriptions of your different talents/gifts and how they can be monetized, identify all of your talents/gifts you can use to positively impact the world around you and then circle them.

5. Examine the list.
   a. If you find there are things on the list that have both a circle and a check, those are the things you should consider utilizing when creating a potential dream to pursue.
   b. If you do not have anything on the list that is both checked and circled, consider the items that are monetizable—the items with a check next to them. If monetizing them will not actively harm people, consider building your dream around those talents.
   c. If you do not see anything that interests you or there are no items that are both monetizable and benign/helpful, repeat the exercise by pairing checked talents/gifts with other things on the list and seeing if new occupation/business ideas emerge.

6. If this exercise does not work the first time, do more research and repeat this exercise until an idea emerges.

Keep in mind that regardless of how random your talent is, somebody has made a successful living off of it. D. L. Hughley said it best, "I used to always run off at the mouth and talk about people. I just didn't know that it would make a living." No matter what your talent is, there is a way to build a dream around it. I know someone who has created lucrative businesses off of something as basic as being a perpetually positive person and knowing how to make other people view the world more positively. There are people who have paired their love of travel with their talent for social media to create millennial-centric travel agencies. There are people who have created successful businesses out of everything from enjoying growing plants to liking to drive long distances to loving to work out and being good at social media. The only limit to what you can achieve with your talents is your imagination.

All that said, people who have dreams, set goals, and attempt to develop a plan can still stagnate for the next three reasons on the list: *Chasing the Perfect Plan, Fear of Failure,* and *Fear of Success.*

Let's start by dispelling the myth of the perfect plan. We have all seen heist movies like *Ocean's Eleven, Den of Thieves*, and *The Italian Job*, where the protagonist creates the perfect plan. The plan is so perfect that it even seems to account for seemingly random occurrences. They even manage to plan the actions of their antagonists, and somehow the bad guy does everything they expected in the exact ways they expected. It's a perfect plan!

> "If you spend too much time thinking about a thing, you'll never get it done."
> Bruce Lee

Sometimes we get caught in a state of analysis paralysis because we believe that we too can create a perfect plan—a plan that will ensure that failure is impossible. We've seen it time and time again in the movies, so surely we can do it, too, right? Planning is a great thing, and all the best accomplishments begin with a plan. Still, you must realize that in the real world, there is no such thing as a perfect plan. The only result of pursuing a perfect plan is a failed accomplishment.

> "The truth is you don't know what is going to happen tomorrow. Life is a crazy ride, and nothing is guaranteed."
> Marshall "Eminem" Mathers III

The only sure way to fail at something is to never try, and if you are spending your energy trying to create a "perfect plan" that accounts for every detail, you are almost certain to never actually start *implementing* the plan. There will always be a new detail to account for or something you can't know at the onset of a major undertaking. If you make beginning your journey contingent on knowing exactly what the outcome will be, you will forever be stuck in the planning phase. Thus, you will never actually accomplish anything.

Put differently, how would you feel if your builder told you that they couldn't start the build until you finalized the carpet in your house? Would it make sense not to start the building process until the color of the kids' rooms' walls were chosen and finalized? This premise is laughable. Homeowners know that any number of things can affect the "final touches" (like paint and flooring) over the course of a lengthy build. The lighting in the house could make certain colors look different, the originally selected fixtures could become unavailable at the time of installation, or you could just suddenly realize that the flooring you thought was pretty now disgusts you. Anybody who has ever gone through the home-building process can tell you that there is really no predicting how things might change but progress must continue nonetheless. In the end, the exterior paint does not affect the wall construction and the showerheads do not affect the house plumbing.

So if the premise of delaying construction of your dream home until you pick the countertops is ridiculous, why is it that we oftentimes delay undertaking our dreams until we know exactly how every minor detail is going to work out?

You tell yourself, "I can't apply to college until I know exactly what career I want." Or "I can't apply for an opportunity until I am absolutely sure I will get it." Or "I can't turn in a job application unless I know it's my dream job." Or "I can't go on a date with someone until I am absolutely certain I will marry them." When planning our lives, we often avoid starting the beginning of a process until we feel we know exactly where it is going to end. We try to analyze and plan every little detail before we start the journey, which is like refusing to start a long road trip unless you know every gas station that you are going to stop at along the way. However, there is no possible way for you to know every pit stop and detour that a thousand-mile journey will have.

Similarly, planning out every detail of your life before you live it is impossible. There is no way to know exactly what tomorrow will hold. Just like you expect that your builder will start constructing the walls of your house even before you know what color you want to paint them, you should expect that you will start working towards your goals even before you know exactly where they will end. You should therefore dispel the notion that a plan can be perfect or that a plan can account for every eventuality. If you have

> "In a world that is changing really quickly, the only strategy that is guaranteed to fail is not taking risks."
> Mark Zuckerberg

established a strong framework, be comfortable with a bit of ambiguity and start building your future.

The other reason why people often get caught in a state of analysis paralysis is to avoid facing their fears. There are two fears that most paralyze us: *the fear of failure* and *the fear of success*.

Fear of failure is something that can often cause analysis paralysis. We are so afraid we may fail that we never try. Worse yet, this kind of analysis paralysis oftentimes results in you eventually just abandoning the pursuit. A perfect example of this is walking up and talking to somebody. Think about the time you really wanted to talk to somebody, but you were afraid to get shot down. You stared and planned and thought and analyzed, but you never actually walked up and initiated a conversation. Eventually, that person left the room, and you told yourself you were better off for not having tried.

> "Throw caution to the wind and just do it."
> Carrie Underwood

I am certain that if you were to take inventory of your life, you would see that many, many times, your fear of failure caused you to never try, whether it was the job you didn't apply for because you didn't think you could get it or the college you didn't apply to because you thought you didn't have a chance at admissions. Maybe it was the mentor you never developed a relationship with because you were afraid to approach them, the person you never went on a date with because you were too afraid to ask them out, or the raise you never got because you didn't want to ask for it. At some point or another in our lives, we have passed up a personal, academic, or professional opportunity because we were so afraid of failure that we didn't try.

When trying to get past the fear of failure, I remind myself of three things:

1. The only sure way to fail at something is to never try. Thus, being overtaken by a fear of failure is the only sure way you will fail to accomplish something.

2. The word "no" never hurt anybody. Most of the time, the failure that we are so afraid of is hearing somebody tell us "no." Oftentimes, we inflate how harmful hearing the word "no" is and we create elaborate scenarios to convince ourselves it will be a great trauma. Nevertheless, at the end of the day, it is just a word. Most of us learned in elementary school that "sticks and stones may break my bones, but words will never hurt me." If you remember that lesson, you will find it laughable to not try for fear of rejection. When looking for an opportunity, you may have to apply dozens if not hundreds of times to get a handful of interviews and eventually one success. Nevertheless, that is a small price to pay for that success, and once you have it, the dozens of "no's" won't matter.

In cases where there is a greater consequence than a simple "no," you may be experiencing "apprehension of failure." Apprehension of failure is something different that we will address later in this chapter. Still, if the only consequence of failure is hearing the word "no," go for it! Remember: nobody will remember those kinds of failures—they will only remember your successes. If you think of the most famously successful people in the world, they have "failed" far more times than they have

> "Don't give up, there's no shame in falling down! True shame is to not stand up again."
> Shintaro Midorima
> (*Kuroko No Basket*)

succeeded. And I put *failed* in quotation marks because nobody cares or even remembers the unsuccessful attempts they made prior to succeeding. Nobody really cares about the thousands of times Edison "failed" when making the lightbulb; nobody bothered to even note the thousands of filaments Lewis Latimer tried before finding the one that made the lightbulb a household item. Nobody remembers the hundreds of shots your favorite basketball player missed in practice. Likewise, nobody is going to care about or remember the rejection letters you got on your way to your dream college, career, or business.

3. If in the moment I am still being paralyzed with fear, I ask myself a question: "On my deathbed, will it haunt me more if I try and fail or never try at all?" Unless I can honestly say "I would regret it more to try and fail," then I will force myself to go for it!

> "I'd rather regret the risks that didn't work out than the chances I didn't take at all."
> Simone Biles

Fear of failure is a concept that most of us are familiar with, but I would imagine that "fear of success" sounds a bit...crazy. Who would be afraid of being successful? But although fear of success seems like an odd concept, it is a fear that most people have experienced. Do you remember being in class and knowing the answer to the question but being too nervous to raise your hand? Or how about that time your boss asked for people to work on a new project, and even though you really wanted to volunteer because it sounded like a perfect fit, you sat quietly in the back of the room? Why were you afraid? What is at the root of this fear?

The first answer that comes to mind is "I was afraid I was wrong" or "I was afraid I would fail." As we previously discussed, sometimes that is a very real fear, but that wasn't why you didn't volunteer. You were certain you knew the answer to that question, and you knew you were the best person for that job. So why didn't you volunteer? Marianne Williamson said it best:

> *"Our deepest fear is not that we are inadequate. Our deepest fear is that we are powerful beyond measure. It is our light, not our darkness, that most frightens us. We ask ourselves, 'Who am I to be brilliant, gorgeous, talented, fabulous?' Actually, who are you not to be? You are a child of God. Your playing small does not serve the world. There is nothing enlightened about shrinking so that other people won't feel insecure around you. We are all meant to shine, as children do. We were born to make manifest the glory of God that is within us. It's not just in some of us; it's in everyone. And as we let our own light shine, we unconsciously give other people permission to do the same. As we are liberated from our own fear, our presence automatically liberates others."*

Put less eloquently, one of our biggest fears is standing out and being different. When you are successful, you stand out. The person who is successfully moving up the ranks will get more and more responsibility at work. The person with more responsibilities will work longer hours and have less time to hang out with their old friends. This principle applies in your professional, academic, and personal lives. The leader has to get there early and leave later, the student trying to get into the best schools has to study harder, and the person trying to avoid prison or the mortuary can't hang out all night on the block.

And it isn't just having less free time—there are other ways you stand out when you are trying to be successful. This concept is perfectly articulated with this truism: "If you want to have something you have never had before, you have to do things you have never done before." If you are working hard to make it to the next level as an athlete, you aren't going to be able to join in with everyone else when they're drinking and eating whatever they want. Whether it is sounding different because you are studying vocabulary to do well in school or prioritizing new things because you are trying to reach a new level, any time you strive for new success, you are going to seem different to the crowd you are used to hanging out with. And that fact is scary.

The reason that being different is scary is because it can go hand-in-hand with the fear of isolation. You start asking yourself questions like:

"What happens if my old friends don't get what I am trying to do?"
"What happens if I don't make new friends where I am trying to go?"
"What if I am not accepted anymore?"
"What if I am not cool anymore?"
"Will they look at me funny?" etc.

These are not trivial fears, and these types of questions follow you from childhood into your professional career. You will find yourself asking similar questions when you transition from being an employee to a manager and/or business owner. You will ask yourself these questions when you transition from being single to being in a committed relationship or when you pursue additional responsibilities (e.g., family, civic leadership, ministry, etc.). All of those transitions carry with them the concern that "Maybe I won't get to keep the same friends or relationships I used to have." Maybe the questions are different and the circumstances are different, but the feeling is the same.

I was blessed—most of my differences are very evident and hard to hide, so I have been considered different, weird, and/or strange my whole life. Throughout the majority of my scholastic career, I was the only or one of the only black kids in my class. Then I had the "audacity" to think it was acceptable to skip grades, so I spent the majority of my scholastic career one to four years younger than everyone else in my classes. Furthermore, I chose engineering and legal professions, so once I entered the world of work, I was always the youngest and typically one of the only black men in my area of the company. Thus, for most of my life, I embraced being different because I had no other choice. When people would ask me how it felt to be different because of my age, ethnicity, occupation, education, etc., I coined the phrase, "I am the only me I have ever been, so it feels normal to me."

Why would I call that a blessing? Well, I assure you that sticking out like a sore thumb regardless of my environment was not always something I viewed as a blessing. I have pretty much gotten picked on since the day I was born, and I walked into most situations knowing I would not quite fit in. So rather than focusing on trying to fit in, I just committed to unapologetically being the best me I could be. Thus, the blessing was that for most of my life, I never had to make the choice to fit in or be different & stand out—it was made for me.

I say "most" of my life because there were definitely times when I found cliques of people I could assimilate into. In those moments where I had to decide between going with a comfortable flow and being true to my ambition, I was forced to make some of the most difficult choices of my life. The time that most illustrates why those types of decisions are difficult was my choice to complete my PhD.

When you graduate from a top-tier law school, it is expected that you will either work for a major law firm or take a prestigious public interest or government job. This is what the vast majority of my classmates did coming out of Harvard Law School, but I went to law school knowing that I had no intention of doing either one—as I said earlier, I knew I was going to go straight from law school into a PhD program. But after three years of belonging to a group of people, the idea of breaking away from that group was scary. And it felt like there were only so many times I could ignore so many people telling me how unnecessary a PhD would be. Did I really want to break away from the crowd and do something different?

> "Follow your passion. Stay true to yourself. Never follow someone else's path unless you're in the woods and you're lost and you see a path. By all means, you should follow that."
> Ellen DeGeneres

There were numerous times where the answer to that question was "no." I sincerely tried to go with the flow and get a job at a great law firm. However, the closer I got to graduation, the more uncomfortable I felt—because my goals were well-grounded in my core motivations, the idea of abandoning them was not an option. Yet, I was still afraid to take the next step. Why?

As I said, this wasn't a fear of failure. There was never a moment where I imagined failing my PhD program. But if not a fear of failure, what was it? It was the fear of being isolated from the people I had grown so close to. I would be on a different trajectory than my friends, which meant I would have less time to see them. I would miss having the opportunity to work with them and have that shared experience of complaining about our cases and meeting up at conventions. Some of my friends even graduated and became roommates, whereas I would be a thousand miles away, both literally and figuratively, pursuing another degree.

Also, what if they were to think I was ridiculous for pursuing an "unnecessary degree"? I didn't want to be the butt of anyone's joke.

Ultimately, there were three things I told myself to get through this transition: 1. *Discomfort is a part of growth,* 2. *It is harder work trying to fit in,* and 3. *Everything isn't for everyone.*

One of the most physically exhausting two weeks of my life occurred very recently. After finishing my last degree, I decided I was going to take some time off to write and get a bit more in shape. I shared these plans with my friend, a former-professional-track-athlete-turned-trainer named Andrea Jackson-Hinds, and she invited me to train with her in Bermuda. For some reason, I thought doing two-a-days with a former heptathlete would be a great way to celebrate my graduation, so I packed my bags.

The first day I trained with her, I threw up and passed out and then came back that afternoon to train again. What made the training program so effective was that it constantly got more challenging. One of her favorite things to tell her clients is to "get uncomfortable." If you can get through a set of one of her circuit workouts and you don't feel discomfort, do more until you do. If ever a circuit got too easy for me, she would create a new one. The rationale is that discomfort is the beginning of growth. If you are stretching your capabilities and reaching for something that you have never achieved before, you are going to feel discomfort along the way.

How does this story relate to you achieving your goals? For those two weeks, I felt like I was going to break,

and I existed in a constant state of discomfort.
Nevertheless, at the end of those two weeks, I had made
more progress towards my fitness goals than I had in the
prior two months. What I learned from that experience—
and what you can learn from my story—was that you can't
become your best while staying in your comfort zone. And
that principle doesn't just apply to workouts.

I understand that crowds are comfortable and that
standing up on your own can be quite *un*comfortable.
However, in order to remain part of the crowd, you are
going to have to constantly diminish yourself so that you
don't stand out. Thus, it is impossible for you to be all that
you were called to be if you are content staying in the
comfort zone of the crowd.

Yes, leaving the comfort zone of the crowd feels
awkward and uncomfortable. Coming out of law school, it
was incredibly uncomfortable to leave guaranteed, high-
paying employment behind to pursue my passion. But
remember that discomfort is the beginning of all growth!
Had I stayed on the comfortable path, I would have only
gained legal experience. By leaving my comfort zone, I
was able to grow as an engineer and businessman while
still growing as a lawyer. The discomfort you feel when
you make yourself stand out and step up to a new level of
responsibility or when you try to achieve a new level of
success is a natural part of the process. If I am not a little
uncomfortable, I know I am probably not doing my best.

I also find that it is always harder to fight against your
true ambition. There is a concept called cognitive
dissonance. Cognitive dissonance is a form of mental stress
you experience when your actions are inconsistent with
your beliefs. In other words, it is more difficult to do
something you don't want to do than it is to do something
you believe in. This is the scientific basis for the old adage,
"If you are doing something you love, you never work a

day in your life." The principle is that if you believe in and love your work, you will find it easier to do.

I have worked jobs where I struggled to get through a basic eight-hour workday, where I felt so tired and questioned whether I could make it through the workweek. While I was pursuing my doctorate degree, I was a full-time student and taking the maximum allowed credit hours every semester. Additionally, I worked 30 to 40 hours per week as legal counsel for a pharmaceutical company while simultaneously working 10 to 20 hours a week as a teaching assistant/lecturer. I did all of this while traveling around the country speaking. There were literally weeks where I worked over 80 hours. Nevertheless, I felt more energetic and happy after a fourteen-hour day of doing things I was passionate about than I did after an eight-hour day of doing what I disliked.

I am sure you have experienced this phenomenon in your personal and professional life. That is not just your imagination! This is the principle of cognitive dissonance at work. Your brain works harder when you do something you hate or when you act against your desires. Simply put, your brain is doing two jobs: your brain is both doing the work and pretending not to hate it. Thus, it is harder for you to do work that you don't believe in and that doesn't help you achieve your goals. So the question I asked myself, and the question I am asking you is, "Why work more to do something you want less?"

Ultimately, of the three realizations I mentioned a few pages ago, the realization that resonated with me the most was that not everything is for everyone. We have all heard that phrase before, yet something we overlook about this phrase is that it implies

> "I'd rather fail being who I am than fail being somebody that they want me to be."
> LeBron James

that everything *is* for someone. When I was struggling to get over my fears about going into my PhD program, the most eye-opening experience I had was having the pleasure of meeting people who were born to stand in a courtroom. Ultimately, meeting some real litigators-in-training was what made me certain that I needed to be on a different path. There is nothing like listening to somebody who has found their purpose in life talk about their job. Everything about the courtroom fascinated them, and they could joyfully ramble on about everything from meeting a client to using an obscure rule of evidence. That is the kind of joy you only experience when you are pursuing your dreams, and I realized *I* wanted that type of joy, too.

Now, when you are pursuing your passion, you are not necessarily going to love everything you do. All of us have to make some sacrifices to achieve our dreams. However, when you are pursuing something you truly believe in and desire, even the mundane and annoying aspects of your job are easier. Seeing people with that type of contentment with their work strengthened my resolve. The crowd I was in had found their passion, and it just happened to be different than mine. Once I made that realization, I decided I needed to pursue something *I* could be that passionate about.

> "You can't make decisions based on fear and the possibility of what might happen."
> Michelle Obama

When you began reading this book, you had a dream you weren't sure if you should dare to dream. By now, you have crystalized that dream into some very concrete goals. Now, you may be like I was as I was going into my last year of law school—you may be letting fear deter you from taking that next big step. I finally did take that leap into the unknown, and three years later, I couldn't imagine having made a different decision. There is nothing I could have achieved in the courtroom that compares to the joy I felt when my committee chair, Dr. César Malavé, shook my hand and called me "Doctor." Ultimately, the joy is worth the risk.

And don't forget how Marianne Williamson's poem ends. When you pursue your passion and let your light shine, you liberate others to do the same. As many times as I have made major transitions, I have always found good people waiting for me in the next stage. And although I sometimes have to leave some people behind, the best ones stick around. When people see you joyfully pursuing your passion, you will find others who want that same happiness. Whether it is new friends at your new level, peers who rise to the occasion with you, or tried-and-true family members who support you no matter what, I guarantee you that whatever isolation you feel will only be temporary.

Despite everything I have said in this chapter, I understand being leery of starting to build towards your dreams. I know that sometimes taking the first steps in a journey can be extremely intimidating, especially if you have set some lofty goals. Coping with the fear of beginning a new chapter in your life or undertaking a new goal is not easy, but it *is* something you can accomplish.

The first step in coping with and overcoming your analysis paralysis is to differentiate between helpful apprehension and debilitating fear. Your apprehension can be healthy, but fear is not. The problem is that it's sometimes hard to distinguish between the two, especially because people use the terms "apprehension" and "fear" synonymously. Additionally, both apprehension and fear result in feeling an uneasy aversion to doing something. I am sure you have a clear understanding of debilitating fear, but what is helpful apprehension?

> "Fear is not evil. It tells you what weakness is. And once you know your weakness, you can become stronger as well as kinder."
> Gildarts Clive
> (*Fairy Tail*)

We have already talked about how everything that makes you uncomfortable is not necessarily bad. Helpful apprehension is one of those useful uneasy feelings. Healthy apprehension is your mind making you aware of a present danger that you may otherwise be ignoring, which helps you prepare for danger. Helpful apprehension makes you take a moment to consider possible negative outcomes and make sure you have prepared for them. It also alerts you to things you might want to work on, protect against, or improve in order to be better positioned for success. In moments where you are doing things like making a risky investment or taking a leap of faith in your career, you should have at least considered the aspects of the risk that make you uneasy.

The exercise I use to help me differentiate between debilitating fear and helpful apprehension is to list out the pros and cons—essentially, it is a modified version of the risk assessment process used in project management. The exercise is as follows:

Exercise 8: Modified Pros and Cons List

1. Draw a vertical line down the middle of the page. Title the first column "Pros" and the second column "Cons."

2. In your Pros column, list out all of the possible benefits of making this decision.

3. In your Cons column, list out all of the possible downsides to making this decision.

4. Now turn the sheet over. This time, draw a line down the middle vertically and across the middle horizontally. What you should have is four rectangles drawn on your paper (i.e., a 2 x 2 grid).

5. Label the first column of your 2 x 2 grid "Pros" and the second column "Cons."

6. In the top row of your Pros column, I want you to list out all of the certain or near-certain positive outcomes from the decision you are making. In this context, "near-certain" can be anything you consider to be more than 90% likely to occur.

   Note that positive and negative outcomes are different than the pros and cons you listed on the front. Outcomes are what is actually happening, pros/cons are how those outcomes will either benefit or harm you. For example, a positive outcome of a heart transplant is that you get a new functional heart. Whereas, the benefits of a new functional heart include that you could extend your life and have more energy. Similarly, a negative outcome of a heart transplant could be a noticeable scar on your chest. A potential harm associated with that scar is a reduced ability to comfortably wear certain clothes.

   This exercise helps you evaluate, both, the potential benefits/harms (the front page) and the potential outcomes (the back page).

7. In the top row of the Cons column, list every certain or near-certain negative outcome of a decision. In this

context, "near-certain" can be anything you consider to be more than 75% likely to occur. The reason this is a lower standard is so that you can more easily identify risks to be mitigated.

8. In the bottom row of the Pros column, write out the best possible scenario you could *reasonably* expect. I emphasize "reasonable" expectations because this should not be the absolute most extreme circumstance you can imagine. For example, it is not a reasonable expectation that going on a school field trip could result in you getting bit by a radioactive spider and becoming a real-life Spiderman.

9. Similarly, in the bottom row of the Cons column, write out the worst possible scenario you could *reasonably* expect. Once again, think about a "reasonable" expectation. Generally, one-in-a-billion scenarios like getting struck by lightning or hit by a meteor shouldn't make your list of worst possible outcomes.

10. Now ask yourself the following questions:
    a. Does the worst possible scenario of my actions (Step 9) result in my or anyone else's serious injury, significant financial loss, incarceration, or death?
    b. Do the cons I wrote in either of the front or back sections outweigh the pros?
    c. Is the result essentially outside of my control, and do I have no ability to diminish the likelihood of any of the negative outcomes listed?

If the answer to any of these questions is "yes," then you are probably experiencing some helpful apprehension that should be addressed. But if the answer to all of these questions is "no," then what you are probably experiencing is debilitating fear. If that's the case, you should ignore your unease and move forward. Later in this chapter, we will talk about some techniques for overcoming fear.

You will never make a worthwhile decision that does not carry with it some inherent risk. The adage "no risk, no reward," is a true statement. The point of this exercise is to make sure that the potential reward outweighs the risk. You can also use this exercise to identify places where risk can be limited or mitigated.

As an example of this exercise at work, let's say you are thinking about going skydiving. Although you think it is going to be fun, you are feeling uneasy about going through with it. Is this uneasiness helpful apprehension or debilitating fear? I completed the previous exercise for going skydiving. Generally, most people who go skydiving feel that the pros outweigh the cons: they get a great conversation starter and will have some exciting videos, and after they get over the initial fear of jumping out of a plane, they find the experience to be quite fun. Additionally, you can do a lot to control how positive your skydiving outcomes will be: you can go through proper training, verify the safety of your parachute, jump while being harnessed to an experienced jumper...the list goes on and on. However, the worst possible outcome of skydiving is death or serious bodily harm.

> "But we also believe in taking risks, because that's how you move things along."
> Melinda Gates

Thus, you can answer "no" to the second two questions, but the answer to the first question is "yes." Therefore, the unease you feel about skydiving is helpful apprehension. This does not mean that you shouldn't skydive. It *does* mean that you should take as many precautions as you can to ensure you will have a positive experience (e.g., train, check reviews on the company, do your safety checks, etc.). Some of your unease should subside when you take those reasonable precautionary steps.

GOING SKYDIVING (front)	
PROS	CONS
Good Conversation Starter	Costs money
Fun experience	Possibly dangerous
Bonding opportunity for me and whoever I go with	Likely going to be frightening
Sense of fulfillment by checking something off of my bucket list	

GOING SKYDIVING (back)	
PROS	CONS
I will get to "fly" fast.	I will be terrified jumping out of the plane, and might have a couple of embarrassing moments as a result.
I will have a cool video and story to share.	
The experience of skydiving is incredibly enjoyable and I have a cool story to tell.	I die because something goes wrong and my parachute does not function properly.

Now consider the example of asking someone to be your mentor. You are in a room, and you see somebody who is in the field you want to work in and doing the kind of work you want to do. Nobody is around them. This is a great opportunity to walk up to them and spark a conversation, yet you have an uneasy feeling that is keeping you frozen. Is this unease helpful apprehension or debilitating fear?

Using the same exercise, we see that there is no real downside to attempting to start a conversation with this person. The only cons to approaching them are that they may tell you "no" and that you may feel embarrassed. The pros are that you are likely to have a good conversation and get valuable information that will help you get closer to your goals. As such, the potential pros far outweigh the cons in every regard.

ASKING SOMEONE TO BE YOUR MENTOR (front)	
PROS	CONS
Possibility that I learn a lot	Feels a little awkward starting a conversation with someone
Likely to get a good conversation	They could say "no"
May get a lifelong mentor	
Exposure to possible job opportunities	
Future Guidance	

ASKING SOMEONE TO BE YOUR MENTOR (back)	
PROS	CONS
I will at the very least get some advice and have a brief conversation.	I will feel awkward starting a conversation with this person.
I get a lifelong mentor and friend who can give me access to life-changing opportunities.	I get told "no" and have to endure some awkwardness as a result.

Additionally, the worst possible scenario does not result in any real harm—it is simply a bit of rejection and an awkward exchange. As I have previously stated, the word "no" is nothing to be afraid of and causes no real harm.

You have an exceptional amount of control over whether or not you have a good conversation with this person and gain a mentor out of this interaction. If you can make a connection with this person and sell them on why you would make a great mentee, you will likely get the positive outcome you are seeking.

This means that the answers to all three of the follow-up questions to this exercise (i.e., 1. *Somebody gets hurt?* 2. *Cons outweigh pros?* 3. *Outcome outside your control?*) are "no." Thus, what you are experiencing is debilitating fear. So IGNORE IT and make a move!

The idea of fear being debilitating is pretty commonplace, but saying "helpful apprehension" may seem odd. Why is apprehension helpful? First and foremost, it can help you avoid pitfalls. We talked earlier about there being multiple routes you can take to get to your dreams. Not all routes are created equal, though. If you dream of owning a multimillion-dollar business, there are immoral, illicit, and illegal manners for achieving that dream. Thus, if you feel uneasy before starting down the very difficult and dangerous path of trying to become the next Pablo Escobar, then that is not fear—that uneasy feeling is helpful apprehension suggesting that you choose a different path.

Helpful apprehension can not only prevent you from starting down the wrong path, it can also keep you on the correct path. We talked earlier about fear of failure causing analysis paralysis. Now let us talk about the apprehension of failure. Whereas fear will paralyze, apprehension will make you proceed cautiously and purposefully towards a destination.

When pursuing your dreams, the negative consequences of failing or giving up should outweigh the benefits of quitting. Thus, you should have an apprehension of failing to achieve your dreams. This apprehension of failure has been something that has stuck with me for my entire life, and I have used it to push myself.

> "I love biting off more than I can chew and figuring it out."
> Jordan Peele

Whether it was telling everyone I knew that I was going to get a PhD before I turned 26, taking over all the legal work for a company of a couple hundred employees the day after passing the bar exam, or even the deadline I gave myself to write this book, I often feel like I'm biting off more than I can chew. In those moments, my apprehension of failing (i.e., the uneasy feeling of letting people down, going back on my word, failing to deliver, etc.) pushes me to keep working towards my goal no matter how much I want to stop. As a result of the desire to avoid failure, I press forward until I achieve success.

Perhaps one of the best examples of this phenomenon was when I started college. I was admitted into college as a 14-year-old high school sophomore, and I started college a week after my 15th birthday. I can still see myself the night before classes started: my fresh 15-year-old-self was sitting in my dorm, thinking, "What the heck did I just do?" I gave up two years of additional preparation for college to live on my own while taking a ridiculous first-year curriculum. What made this feeling worse was when I sat in my room and calculated that I could have graduated undergrad in about the same time had I stayed in high school. Between having an additional two years of AP credits and dual-enrollment courses, I would have started college as at least a sophomore. The only thing that kept me from getting my refund and taking myself back to the less-risky path of finishing high school was a healthy apprehension of failure.

People in my hometown had made such a big deal about me starting college early that I ended up making the local news. Additionally, all of my family and friends knew I was starting college early. I knew that if I flunked out or quit, doing so would hurt my reputation and make it harder for me to get support from people later on. Plus, failing at such an opportunity could have made it harder for me to get into good colleges later. Because I wanted to avoid those very negative outcomes, I worked harder than I had ever worked before to do exceptionally well.

> "If everything was perfect, you would never learn and you would never grow."
> Beyoncé Knowles

It helps to have a healthy apprehension of failure to push you to avoid it at all costs. Note that avoiding failure does not always mean avoiding setbacks. Do not interpret this chapter as a license to boorishly pursue things to the detriment of yourself or others. Success and failure are not measured by the outcomes of each occurrence, competition, or day—they are measured by the overall trajectory of your life. We all experience losses and setbacks, but you only fail if you do not learn from them and come back stronger the next time. As will be discussed in later chapters, being unable to accept a loss and move forward puts you on a long-term path to destruction even if you experience short-term success.

While a lot of apprehensions signal things you should avoid, experiencing helpful apprehension does not always mean that you should not go through with an action. However, experiencing apprehension *does* always mean that you must carefully and critically assess whether or not this decision is worthwhile. In situations where you find the risk is worth proceeding, proceed aware and with caution. Think of surgery. The risk of serious bodily harm is always present when undergoing a surgical procedure, but nevertheless, that risk should not stop you from engaging in life-saving treatments. The risk of death is always a possible outcome when a firefighter or police officer responds to a 911 call. However, that risk is something these brave men and women in uniform accept.

Accepting risk does not mean ignoring danger. That is why firefighters and police officers train constantly—whenever possible, they want to minimize risk to themselves and others. Similarly, whenever reasonably possible, try to limit the risks to yourself and others that your decisions would/could cause. If you have accepted the risk of being an athlete in an extreme sport, wear proper protective gear. If you decide to take risks in the world of business, have some savings and make sure to limit your legal liability whenever possible. When you engage in risk-mitigating measures, your apprehension will subside if not disappear altogether.

Now let's talk about fear. When you find that your uneasiness is debilitating fear instead of helpful apprehension, how do you deal with it? Just acknowledging that you are hesitating out of fear means that you have already overcome the first step. You cannot conquer an enemy you are unwilling to face. Make no mistake; fear is the enemy of your success. Once you have acknowledged that you are afraid of something, you can work to overcome it.

Fear is our natural response to the unknown in the same way that holding your breath is the natural response to straining to lift something heavy. Think about it. Nobody ever teaches you to hold your breath when you lift, yet everyone does it. Holding your breath is incredibly unhealthy and counterproductive when trying to exert yourself physically, yet it feels comfortable to give in to the impulse to do so. The same logic applies to fear. We are not taught to fear the unknown and it is counterproductive for us to do so. And just like a weightlifter can learn how to overcome the impulse to hold their breath when lifting, you can train yourself to work through your fear.

Think about your first experiences in a swimming pool. Some people are able to leap immediately into the deep end and either sink or swim. The sink-or-swim method of coping with fear is, essentially, to completely immerse yourself in whatever makes you afraid. Imagine someone who is afraid to leave their comfort zone. The sink-or-swim method of conquering that fear would be for them to move to a completely new area and acclimate themselves to it. This method has its benefits; the primary benefit is that it can result in you accepting your fear in a seemingly instantaneous manner.

However, this method for coping with fear has a major downside. In a sink-or-swim situation, if you swim, great! But there is always the possibility that you will become overwhelmed and sink. Using the previous example, if the person moves to a new area and conquers their fears, the method is a success. Conversely, if they fail to conquer their fears, they will be stuck with a lease or mortgage in a place that makes them miserable.

> "Life opens up opportunities to you, and you either take them or you stay afraid of taking them."
> Jim Carrey

The other danger associated with the sink-or-swim method is that failure oftentimes leaves you worse off than when you started. The people who get thrown into the deep end and fail to figure out how to swim oftentimes find the experience traumatizing. Similarly, if you immerse yourself in your fear and fail to conquer it, the experience can heighten the debilitating nature of your fear. Because of this potential negative outcome, I would only recommend the immersive sink-or-swim approach if you are dealing with extreme time sensitivity or an opportunity that might only come once or twice in a lifetime. If that is the case, throw yourself into the "deep end" and fight through your fear.

A practical example of me engaging in the sink-or-swim method of conquering my fears happened when I was offered my first job out of law school. I was hired to be Assistant General Counsel for a pharmaceutical company based in Texas, and as such, I was going to be responsible for all day-to-day legal matters for the company. The idea was terrifying. If I screwed something up, hundreds of people's livelihoods could be impacted, millions of dollars could be lost, and—because we were making pharmaceuticals meant to combat pandemics—lives could be lost. There was nothing I had done in law school that had truly prepared me for this level of responsibility. To make matters worse, I was in school full-time working on my PhD.

Some aspects of accepting the job gave me reasonable apprehension. I addressed those circumstances to the best of my ability and still felt uneasy. That is when it became apparent that I was just plain afraid. Still, this was truly a once-in-a-lifetime opportunity that lawyers typically don't get unless they have been practicing law for at least a decade. Knowing that fact, declining or delaying this opportunity was not an option, and despite my fear, I accepted the job.

When using the sink-or-swim method, you overcome fear by being too busy to think about being afraid. For me, I didn't have time to be afraid because I was too busy managing my company's legal department and doing my part to get us acquired by an international corporation. And I did all of this while being in school full-time. I didn't think about how afraid I should have been until I was explaining my job to somebody at the banquet we later held to celebrate our company's acquisition. At that point, the job was no longer terrifying because I had already been doing it for over a year.

A more practical approach to learning how to cope with fear is the way that most of us learned how to swim, in an incremental fashion. Typically, you are taught how to swim by spending a day getting comfortable floating in the water; then, the next day, you work on your kicking; after that, you work on your arm movements. You continue to learn small lessons that, when put together, result in you swimming. Likewise, if you are afraid to pursue a particular goal, break it up into incremental activities that will prepare you for the overall goal: each day, pick a couple of very manageable tasks to complete that don't scare you. With each activity you complete, you get closer and closer to achieving your goal. Eventually, you will have progressed so close to your goal that it will no longer intimidate you to pursue it.

For example, if your goal is to start a bakery, the prospect of actually starting a business might be too daunting; instead, pursue smaller incremental tasks. Commit to look up three possible locations for your bakery each day, bake a certain number of pastries each week, or commit to practicing and refining a new recipe each day. After you get more confident, set more aggressive interim tasks, like winning a baking competition, or visiting potential bakery locations in your area. The objective is to make sure that every day you keep progressing through small, non-threatening steps that perpetually push you towards your goal. As you progress closer and closer to your goal, the tasks you choose will get bigger and bigger. Eventually, you will have done so much related to opening your bakery that the idea of just going ahead and opening the shop will feel more inevitable than scary.

For this exercise, the plan you created in the previous chapters will be helpful, because it will give you a roadmap of smaller incremental goals you can work towards. In that detailed plan, find something you are not afraid to do and do it! Do another task the next day and another the next day. Make sure that every day you accomplish a step towards your goal. Keep progressing a day at a time until your fear subsides.

"The road to success and greatness is always paved with consistent hard work. Outwork your competitors, be authentic and above all else... chase your greatness." Dwayne "The Rock" Johnson

Chapter 7:
Be Flexible but Uncompromising

Now that you have a plan you are working, be mindful that your plan is not set in stone. As you learn more and do more, you should periodically revise your plan. As previously discussed, your plan is a living document, which means it should consume information, grow, and adapt to changing circumstances. This requires you to be flexible in your planning. However, you should NEVER compromise your core values (i.e., your code of conduct and the principles that dictate your morality). This chapter is going to give you some tools to be flexible without compromising who you are.

Life is unpredictable—no matter how good of a planner you are there, will always be a contingency you didn't account for. In engineering, we call this the N+1 Rule. The rule says that no matter how well you plan for every possible situation (i.e., Situation 1 through Situation N), there will always be at least one situation you didn't anticipate (i.e., Situation N+1). This rule means

> "Everyone has a plan 'till they get punched in the mouth."
> Mike Tyson

that every system or plan—no matter how well designed— will face a situation that had not been previously thought of by the planner. The N+1 rule comes up when designing factories. The idea is that there is a limit to how much a logical person can plan for completely random occurrences and/or the actions of somebody behaving wholly illogically. Most engineering systems can easily handle the things we plan for; however, the truly successful ones will find a way to handle unexpected things, too.

Now apply this N+1 rule to your life. Think about all the things that influence your life that you have no control over or warning about: *storms shutting down cities, random illness, elections, births, deaths, random meetings, etc.* Right now, someone you have never met is making a decision that will positively or negatively impact your life. This is precisely why the "perfect plan" can never exist in the real world. That fact isn't something to be bothered by or even concerned about—it is just a fact to accept. Therefore, like the engineering system, the success of your planning will not be based on how well you respond to planned occurrences; that's easy. Your success will largely be determined by how well you can adapt to *un*planned situations.

When I began my academic journey, my plan was to get a medical degree so that I could conduct medical research. As I progressed through school, I realized something about myself I hadn't known: I hate hospitals with a passion! I love the work that is done in them, and I think that healing people is one of the noblest pursuits someone can undertake. Nevertheless, my spirit sinks whenever I set foot in a hospital.

Hating to be in a hospital is a horrible trait for a medical student. Had I adhered to my original plan, I would have spent years dreading the simple act of going to class. Imagine trying to manage the natural anxiety of taking a test while being irritated by the entirety of your surroundings. Needless to say, this was an unexpected circumstance that could have derailed my progress. How did I cope? I was flexible and adapted my plan to exclude a medical degree.

That did not mean that I gave up on my desire to perform medical research. I kept the spirit of my goal in mind while changing my plan. Instead of pursuing a mechanical or electrical engineering degree in undergrad, I added a bioengineering degree to my plan. By majoring in bioengineering, I was able to do quite a bit of medical research in undergrad.

> "Adapt what is useful, reject what is useless, and add what is specifically your own."
> Bruce Lee

Whenever you make changes to your plan, make sure that you keep the core components of your dream intact and that all of the changes you make are still well-grounded in your core motivations. In this context, I was flexible enough to change my pursuits to something else in the medical field. However, I did not compromise the core aspects of my dream to help people, improve health, and gain the title of Doctor. Additionally, my new pathway was well-grounded in the motivation to be able to improve my family's access to healthcare and to care for them long-term.

Also, despite the foreboding tone of the beginning of this chapter, life can be unexpectedly good. Do not be so fixated on completing your plan that you miss opportunities to achieve your major goals and dreams. Remember your values, core motivations, and dreams, and take opportunities that allow you to get closer to these desires.

For example, let's say you are someone who has the dream of becoming a CEO. As part of this dream, you have set the goals of becoming a department manager, a district manager, a regional manager, a vice president, and a Chief Operating Officer (COO). By now, you have laid out a detailed plan of how you are going to accomplish each of those tasks, and you are working that plan. After a few years of being a stellar department manager, one of your product lines becomes the biggest product in the company. As a result of this success, you are given the opportunity to be a special assistant to your company's Chief Technology Officer (CTO); the CTO (like the COO) is a position that reports directly to the CEO. What do you do?

This seems like a no-brainer—you take the job! Yet a lot of us hesitate when confronted with these kinds of unexpected opportunities, or we shy away from them altogether to try to preserve the plan. Be open to accepting unexpected opportunities.

This does not mean that you should pursue *any* opportunity you are given—some opportunities are detours rather than shortcuts. In general, be open to unexpected opportunities if they help you get closer to your dream (e.g., shortcuts). Clearly, the opportunity to work directly with the CTO is a wonderful stepping-stone to eventually becoming the CEO. However, most of the opportunities you encounter will not be so cut-and-dried. To assess the difference between a detour and a shortcut, you must ask yourself two simple questions: *"Does this opportunity lead me further from my dream?"* and *"Does this opportunity lead me closer to my dream or one of my major goals?"*

> "Every day is different; you never know what to expect, and you have to be ready to pivot on a dime."
> Kris Jenner

Why is it important to ask both questions? Aren't they the same question? No, they aren't—the questions are unique and equally important. Anything that you know will actively take you further away from your dream is something you should not do. So if the answer to the first question is "yes," then this opportunity is a detour. What does it mean when the answer to the first questions is "no"? That depends on the answer to the second question (*"Does this opportunity lead me closer to my dream or one of my major goals?"*). When the answer to this second question is "yes," then the opportunity is an unexpected shortcut. Use the methods we discussed in the chapter about creating a plan to make a new plan that includes this unexpected shortcut. If the answers to both questions are "no," then the opportunity is neither a shortcut nor a detour—it falls into the third category of unexpected opportunities, the category called a "time-sink."

Time-sinks are innocuous activities that neither benefit nor harm your progress. The problem is that (as the name implies) they waste time! Typically, time-sinks are things that should be avoided unless they are part of your reward system. We will discuss reward systems in later chapters.

When deciding whether something is a shortcut, detour, or time-sink, keep relationship-building in mind. I want to caution against dismissing opportunities just because the benefit to you is not immediately apparent. Even if the opportunity itself does not necessarily get you closer to your goal, it may get you "relationship capital" with people who can help you achieve your goals.

Later, we will talk in greater detail about relationship capital and team members (e.g., coaches, mentors, sponsors, cheerleaders, etc.), but for now I will say that if a trusted advisor, mentor, or sponsor presents you with an opportunity or asks you to do something, strongly consider it before turning them down. And when considering whether something helps you reach your goals, make sure to consider how building goodwill can help you achieve your goals.

This is not an exact science, and it is definitely something that you will learn with time. During my first summer in law school, I worked for a major law firm in their intellectual property department. The head of that practice area was trying to grow the department and was looking for new lawyers to help him with that expansion. He was excited to bring me on board and "show me the ropes." This attorney was someone who could have been a solid mentor and potential sponsor (i.e., someone who could have given me access to high-level opportunities). I, being the naïve 20-year-old that I was at the time, did not yet know the importance of networking events. So I worked late and skipped social events that would have allowed me to get to know him better and meet more of my potential clients and coworkers. The events that I skipped included one that the head of the IP department hosted at his home.

These networking events were not required or necessary for my job. They did not lead me closer to or further from my goals, which essentially made them a time-sink. So was it a wise decision for me to skip those networking events?

NO! Although the events were not directly beneficial, they were also not harmful. Had I gone, I would have built relationship capital with several potential mentors and could have gained a great sponsor. Those relationships could have been invaluable resources that could/would have helped me achieve my goals. For that reason alone, skipping those events was an example of a missed opportunity.

What were the consequences of missing these opportunities? First, I conveyed to my mentor/sponsor that I didn't really want his guidance. Next, it conveyed to the rest of my coworkers that I was not serious about advancement in the organization. And ultimately, those perceptions cost me an opportunity to work with that organization again the following summer. Working with them further could have been a shortcut to achieving some of my other goals. Thus, skipping those networking events was an example of a potential shortcut that I missed out on.

On the other hand, not all opportunities that are presented to you by a mentor or sponsor are automatically worth pursuing. For example, while I was in my PhD program, one of my advisors presented me with a research opportunity. It was a large multifaceted research project where I would work with a national team. This project could have lasted for years and resulted in multiple publications. In some regards, it was a great opportunity for me to get my name out there more.

However, my goal was not to acquire notoriety or more publications. Also, if I had taken advantage of this opportunity, the advisor would have likely wanted me to finish the research project before I would have been allowed to graduate. My primary goal was to graduate in a timely fashion. If I was going to stick to my timeline and fulfill my dream, I needed to complete my PhD program in three years. Furthermore, the longer I was in school, the longer I would be accruing interest on my law school loans and the longer I would have to delay making significant income. That additional debt would have a negative impact on my ability to effectively pursue some of my entrepreneurial endeavors. Despite how much of an opportunity the research project could have been, it would have likely taken me further away from my goals and dream. Thus, I made the correct decision in turning it down.

You will have to make tough decisions like this periodically, too. You are ultimately the sole person responsible for your success, and you must take an active role in pursuing and protecting your dreams. Nevertheless, just because you make the correct decision does not mean it is without consequences.

It would be foolish to expect that my decision to reject the opportunity to work on my advisor's research program would have no impact on my relationship with that advisor. Any time you reject a request or recommendation from someone, you risk damaging your relationship with them. So you must give careful consideration to how you say "no" and do your best to mitigate hurt feelings and/or negative backlash.

In this particular situation, there was no way I could have tactfully declined without damaging the relationship (although I sincerely tried). I understood that risk even before I made the decision. So not only did I have to decide that that project was something I could succeed without, but I also had to decide that that advisor was somebody that I could survive having a damaged relationship with. My assessment was that potentially damaging my relationship with this particular advisor would do less to delay my graduation than participating in the extensive research project. I did not make that decision lightly. And even though it was the correct decision, my relationship with that advisor was still irreparably harmed.

It will not be the case that every time you tell a mentor "no," your relationship will be irreparably harmed (or even that it will be harmed at all). I can think of plenty of times that I have successfully declined a recommendation or request from a mentor and had no issues. However, you always must take into account the possible relationship strain when you weigh the pros and cons of turning someone down.

"Take chances, make mistakes, get messy!" Ms. Frizzle (*The Magic School Bus*)

The main point of this chapter is that plans can be fluid as long as you do not compromise yourself, your values, or your dreams. Once you internalize that you can change your plans, there is another added benefit: by internalizing the fact that you have the ability to change your mind, you become more comfortable starting to build towards your dreams and accomplishments. The previous chapter talked about analysis paralysis and how one major cause of it is a false belief that you can create the perfect plan. Thus, part of the reason we get caught in analysis paralysis is that we assign undue weight to our early decision-making. In other words, we put the weight of our future actions and decisions solely on our current selves, which is an unreasonable pressure. Just because you make choices about your field of study/work, career, or industry does not mean that you can't choose something else later. When you realize this fact, you remove some of the undue pressure of early planning and are more willing to start working towards your dreams.

I want to reiterate this point for the students reading this material. While in high school and college, you have the latitude to try new things and find & pursue passions you might not have even known you had. However, one of the largest stumbling blocks to this personal exploration is the belief that every career decision carries the weight of the world. What you major is in college doesn't have to be what you do for the rest of your life, and your first occupation does not have to be your future career.

Your college major should be able to set you up for a safe, salaried career that can take care of you. While in college, you should be constantly advancing towards graduating with such a major. However, that doesn't mean you can't try out other pathways or pursue different dreams than what you majored in. Utilize your electives and get work experience in a variety of disciplines. Every class you take and every job you work doesn't have to be your true calling! I strongly encourage you to try things outside of your comfort zone, because you might find things that you never thought you would love.

Although my undergraduate major was in biomedical engineering, I very rarely do any of the lab or technical work I was trained to do. Nevertheless, the degree provided me with invaluable training, access to new opportunities, and a career to fall back on should my aspirations fail. Similarly, other well-known business owners, entertainers, politicians, comedians, doctors, actors, pilots, artists, athletes, and a host of other professionals have attained engineering degrees without intending to be engineers. All of them realized that the major you pick when you are 20 years old does not define who you are for the rest of your life.

And when thinking about plan changes, remember that it is never too late! Some people have become professional athletes in a sport they didn't start playing until college. Some people didn't get their billion-dollar business idea until they were in their forties or fifties. As long as you have breath in your body, you have the ability to pursue something new and exciting. Be open to the twists and turns your life may take. And whenever you find a new passion, an additional new dream, or a new goal, go back and set S.M.A.R.T. Goals, plan, and start building!

When I talk about being flexible but uncompromising, the primary focus of the chapter thus far has been on not compromising your dreams and making sure to keep focused on your destination even when the route changes. But "be flexible but don't compromise" has another important meaning. Similar to how your plan can be challenged by unexpected circumstances, you and your character will be tested in the most unpredictable ways. We talk more about the value of your reputation in other chapters, but it is a point worth reiterating here.

Understand that "A good name is more desirable than great riches; to be esteemed is better than silver or gold." (Prov. 22:1 NIV) The reason your reputation is so valuable is because your reputation can be converted into tangible resources and opportunities; whereas, money and resources cannot buy a good reputation.

How can your reputation be converted into tangible resources? Every time someone gives you a loan, helps you develop an idea, or recommends you for an opportunity, that is your reputation being converted into something tangible. Your credit score is the perfect embodiment of this concept.

Your credit score is your reputation for paying back your debts. Someone with a high credit score has a good reputation for paying back their debts. Whereas a person with a low credit score has a bad or unknown reputation (i.e., they don't have a credit history, so nobody knows if they will pay back their debts on time). One of the greatest things you can do for your long-term wealth is to have a high credit score. Why?

When you have a high credit score, banks and lenders give you a low-interest rate whenever you borrow money. In some cases, you can even make money by borrowing it because the interest rate is so low or you effectively use cash-back incentives. And at any point you want, you can convert the reputation associated with your good credit score into thousands if not hundreds of thousands of dollars (e.g., credit cards, home loans, car loans, personal loans, cash advances, etc.).

Similarly, your words have no intrinsic value—saying "I will pay you back" or "I will owe you one" is not valuable to someone unless a strong reputation is backing those words. When backed by a good reputation, saying "I will pay you back" can literally be worth millions of dollars to someone. For this reason, a good reputation is the most valuable thing you can have.

Your credit score is an example of converting your good reputation into money. Your good reputation can also open the door to new opportunities. Part of how you get jobs, are admitted into universities, and obtain any number of other opportunities is based on your reputation. How good are your references? What do people have to say about you when they recommend you? What information is publicly available about you? The answer to those questions is your reputation opening (or closing) doors for you.

Your reputation can precede you in a good way or a negative way—the choice is yours. Your reputation is something that money cannot buy, yet it has the ability to gain you access to a lot of money.

For this reason, you should never compromise your core values (e.g., your principles, ideals, and integrity) to attain a shortcut to your dreams or goals. There are numerous paths to get to your goals; if one route closes, you can easily find another. However, once you ruin your reputation, it is nearly impossible to reestablish it.

We can think of dozens of people who have attained short-lived fame and fortune based on cheap gimmicks, selling out their communities and families. Or people who have prostituted themselves (both figuratively and literally) to get a few minutes in the spotlight. When you read those last sentences, you probably thought of a few people who fall into one of those categories. What most of those people have in common is that they are neither famous nor fortunate right now. Keep that in mind when making decisions about your future.

Once your integrity has been called into question or your reputation is tarnished, you will never completely get the stain out. I cannot emphasize enough the importance of staying true to your core values. Even when it is inconvenient or you think nobody is paying attention, integrity is a major key to long-term success. The main reason is this: no matter how well you think you can hide your deeds, what is done in darkness has a tendency to come to light at some point.

A test I use to see whether or not I should avoid doing something is to ask the following questions:

> *"Could I justify this to my ten-year-old self?"*
> *"Could I justify this to my mom?"*
> *"Will I be able to justify this to God on my day of judgment?"*
> And *"Would all three approve?"*

The idea behind this exercise is to try to curtail your ability to justify wrongdoing. The *ten-year-old you* represents a check on your ability to rationalize your actions. Whenever you have a conversation with a child, they are constantly asking why: "Why you are doing something?" and "Why does it

> "It takes many good deeds to build a good reputation, and only one bad one to lose it."
> Benjamin Franklin

make sense?" If you iteratively ask yourself why, you force yourself to get to the bedrock of your actions, outcomes, and intentions. And a child's cut-and-dried understanding of morality will generally tell you the truth regardless of how nice or appropriate that truth is.

When thinking about having to explain yourself to a child, you are forced to think about how your actions may positively or negatively impact the world. This is essentially comparing your actions to your most fundamental core values without rationalizing or making excuses. Can your actions hold up against those fundamental core values? Are you hurting people, are you helping people, or are you doing some combination of the two?

The *parent* in this exercise represents the person who knows when you are lying to yourself and them. This is the person who knows all of your "tells" and is going to force you to be 100% honest with them when they talk to you. They know enough about you to help you find your true expectations. When you talk to your parents, they are going to force you to be honest with yourself.

Trying to explain yourself to a parent means having to be honest. Growing up in my house, lying was—and still is—the worst offense you could commit. It was understood that lying about something drastically increased the severity of your punishment. So when I think about talking to my mom, I think about being honest to a fault. Are you being 100% honest about your assessment of what you are doing?

God represents someone who knows the inner workings of your heart and your true intentions. The reason this is important is because your true intentions have a tendency to manifest in your actions. For example, take a situation where someone is helping you, but they hate you and want to see you fail. Their true intention in helping you is to have a "front-row seat" for your failure. Eventually, you and other people will notice this person relishing in your setbacks and will react accordingly. Now that person will have a reputation as a hateful saboteur.

Your intentions are going to motivate your actions, and they *will* manifest themselves. For that reason, do not put yourself in a situation where your good actions are in conflict with negative intentions.

The last question of "Would all three approve?" is also an important question to ask. Since you aren't really going to be able to ask God or your ten-year-old self and you might not be willing or able to ask your parent, you should think critically about what someone would say in response to your explanation. Also, it may help to consult trusted friends and advisors (i.e., your coaches). These three individuals—God, your parent, and your younger self—have a clear picture of your core values and moral standards. With that knowledge, would they agree that your actions are justifiable and morally acceptable?

Note that this exercise does not need to be taken literally. For example, some of us have never met our parents, or perhaps the parents we know are not the best authority on moral character. The exercise is my attempt at finding the things that best represent my morality, honesty, and integrity and then measuring my actions against them.

Thus, the exercise is my attempt at honestly asking myself four questions:

> *"Is this a moral action that will have a positive impact on the people and world around me?"*
>
> *"Am I being honest with myself about the outcomes and my intentions?"*
>
> *"Are my intentions good? Is it correct to say that I do not have an ulterior motive that might derail the good I am doing?"*
>
> *"Would other reasonable people agree?"*

I know that I am unequivocally staying true to my core values if I can emphatically answer "yes!" to all four questions. If, for any reason, you encounter a situation where you feel that you are unable to honestly answer "yes" to all four questions, then I strongly recommend reconsidering your choices.

> "Sometimes people can't control what life does, but the thing they can control is their choices. So as long as you are able to live with the choices you make, then it's all good. I just hope that your vision is clear and you made the right one."
> C. Dean Wilson

Chapter 8:
Delayed Gratification

Delayed gratification is the act of not giving yourself or allowing yourself to have something until it is the most beneficial and least costly. Another way of looking at it is that you resist the temptation to attain smaller, more immediate rewards so that you may attain a greater reward later. I have found that I am able to get so much more from life when I am willing to be patient. Delayed gratification is a tool that will allow you to have and accomplish more in life, but it isn't always an easy tool to master. Three pitfalls make delayed gratification difficult.

The first pitfall to avoid is mistaking things you *want* for things that you *need*. How many times have you told yourself, "I need a new [blank]?" Whether it is a nicer phone, a newer car, new shoes, or more money, we are quick to categorize something as a need. When we do that, we send the message to ourselves that we must get this thing at any cost or else our survival will be threatened. But how often is that actually true?

Ultimately, you need very few things to survive: food, water, shelter, health, and safety. Unless something affects your ability to acquire one of these things for yourself or your family in a very direct fashion, it is a "want" and not a "need." Sometimes it is hard to distinguish between the two. When determining whether or not something is a need, ask the question, "If I do not have this, will it negatively impact my or my family's ability to live, be healthy, or be safe?" If the answer is "no," then it is something you want and not something you need.

The reason why this distinction is important is that while *wants* can be delayed, *needs* cannot. Thus, by correctly differentiating between what you need and what you want, you can more efficiently use your time, energy, and money. Time, energy, and money are limited resources that we often don't have enough of. As a rule, you never want to spend too much time, energy, or money on what you want and then not have enough of one of those resources remaining to get everything that you actually need.

Sometimes this rule can result in some tough decisions. When I say "want" versus "need," the first things people think about are situations like buying new shoes versus paying the rent. Those are the easy decisions, but sometimes differentiating between a need and a want can be tough. If you are like me, you feel a "need" to help others. Although it is valiant to help others, it is important to understand that helping others is actually a want and not a need. Don't get me wrong—I believe we are all called to help others. However, if we don't proactively address our own needs, we can't help anyone else.

This is the reason why airlines tell you to put on your oxygen mask before assisting others. Let's say you try to assist someone else with their mask, but you faint during the process because of a lack of oxygen. You needed that oxygen to survive. Now you won't be able to secure the mask of the person you were helping AND you won't have anybody to assist with your mask. By failing to prioritize your need for oxygen, you actually put both you and the other passenger in a worse situation.

During the finals week of my fourth year of college, I spent a lot of my energy and time tutoring other people. My rationale was that my test was on the last day of finals week, and because they needed help, I needed to help them. Once I had gotten everybody through their tests, I barely had any time or energy left for my own studies. I needed to do well in that class, and I had wanted to help my friends with their finals as well. But because I thought I "needed" to help them, I didn't have enough time or energy to get through the studying I needed to do. And, just as in the oxygen mask example, although I could help them study, none of my friends had the ability to tutor or help me with my class.

What would have happened if I hadn't passed that class? Failing it could have delayed my graduation from undergrad and harmed my ability to get into law school. I would have had to take a greater course load to make up for the failed class and bring my grade point average (GPA) back up. In which case, during the next semester, I would not have had time to do as much tutoring and peer mentoring. Thus, I would have been less able to help people in the future and be further from achieving my dream.

Sure enough, I bombed the test. I started out with four days to study for the final, but helping other people left me with only a day to study. It wasn't enough time to review all of the material, so I unambiguously failed the exam even with a curve. Luckily, even though I bombed that exam, I had done very well in my classes throughout the rest of the semester. So, despite my final-exam grade, I did well enough in my other classes to make it out of that semester with my GPA intact.

It is important to realize that not everything you want is selfish or petty. You can want some pretty great things! I want to contribute positively to world health and the education of young people. But if I don't prioritize being healthy and well-educated myself, how can I heal or educate others? By addressing my needs first, I ensure that I have the ability to address the needs of others. Similarly, you may want to do some great things, but make sure that you are not neglecting your needs in the process.

The second pitfall to avoid is failing to realize the difference between delayed gratification and deprivation. We oftentimes think of "delayed gratification" as if it is us telling ourselves "maybe later," which is adult-speak for "never." We believe that if we don't get something now, we just won't get it; thus, we adopt the "now or never" mentality. Saying "maybe later" is not delayed gratification—it is essentially deprivation.

But delayed gratification is not a maybe, it is a definitive "yes!" in the future. This means that at some point, you *are* going to get the thing you want, but you are going to wait until the cost is less substantial. Therefore, instead of saying "maybe later," you are unequivocally telling yourself "definitely later!"

> "There are still many causes worth sacrificing for, so much history yet to be made."
> Michelle Obama

I do not believe that it is necessary to lead a deprived life. I fully expect to have everything I have fantasized about having and do all the stuff I have daydreamed about doing. I have a nice list of achievements I plan to make, places I plan to travel, and adventures I will have. Rest assured that I am slowly but surely checking items off of the list. Within reason, you also should expect to have the things you want. The point of delayed gratification is to sacrifice a bit now so that you can have a lot later.

I love movies of all kinds: comedies, action, anime, westerns, sports movies, biopics, etc. When I was in junior high, I made a list of movies and television shows I wanted to own. This was prior to the existence of live streaming and the prevalence of online portals. So, if I wanted to see movies, I had to either rent them or own them, and for some of the television series boxed sets, renting was not an option. At the time, I didn't have a lot of money, and some of the boxed sets on my list were hundreds of dollars. Nevertheless, over the course of the next eight years, I systematically acquired all of the items on my list (plus a lot more). By waiting, some of the boxed sets became significantly less expensive to own, and I gave myself time to get better jobs and save more money. Even though the process took years, I made sure that I got everything I wanted.

It doesn't always need to take that long to get what you want—sometimes it can be as simple as waiting a few months for the beta version of a new device or for the year-end clearance event for a new car. Especially when you are talking about depreciating assets (e.g., cars, cellphones, games, devices, electronics, etc.) that lose value over time, waiting a little longer to get something can save you a significant amount of money. Additionally, sometimes you are able to attain something that is higher-quality or more abundant by waiting. However, the most important thing to remember is that you are delaying, *not* depriving.

This brings me to the last pitfall to avoid. The main reason so many of us believe that delayed gratification means deprivation is because we don't make a plan to get what we want. You can't expect that if you don't have the funds for a nicer/new car today, then without any additional effort or forethought you are going to have that money in the future. You can't expect that somehow you are going to get a lower interest rate than the subprime mortgage offers you are getting today if you aren't proactively working to improve your credit score or save for the future. Similarly, you are not going to get that degree in the future if you aren't even enrolled in classes or currently making a plan to be enrolled in classes very soon. If you want delayed gratification to work, use the steps in this book to make a plan so that you know how the delay will be beneficial.

Yes, the focus of this book is heavily geared towards giving you the tools to achieve major dreams, but the same tools apply to achieving short-term goals. Thus, clearly articulate and understand how you will get to what you want at a lower personal cost. Turn those wants into short-term S.M.A.R.T. Goals, create a plan, and start working.

Using the example of the list of movies and television shows I wanted, I developed a plan for how I would acquire more money to be able to buy them. Additionally, I kept a continuous watch over when prices were coming down on the items on my list. Over the course of that eight-year period, I made sure I continually progressed towards my goal. By the time I acquired the last item on my list, it had reduced in price from over $120 to less than $30.

However, I was only willing to wait that long because I had a plan in place to assure myself that one day I would complete my list. Without that plan, delaying gratification would have been more difficult, and I might have prioritized these particular wants over my needs. I could have easily blown several paychecks

> "Discipline is just choosing between what you want now and what you want most."

acquiring those movies and TV shows, and that would have left me unable to get everything I actually needed.

Exercising the discipline to delay gratification does not just apply to getting things you want—it can also be applied to your long-term goals. Anything worth having in life is going to require some sacrifices. Nothing in life is free, and you will either pay for it now or later. Anybody you see "living it up" and having a great time is either cashing in an investment or running up a bill. So it is up to you to decide if you want to put in the work now and spend the rest of your life reaping the benefits or have all of your fun now and spend the rest of your life working off that debt.

I travel extensively around the country speaking with high-school and college-age young people. A question that always comes up is the question of having fun while in college: *"Can you still have fun while pursuing your passion?"*

This is something we will talk about in greater detail in the "Celebrate EVERY Victory" chapter, but the short answer is "yes." Yes, you can and should have fun! Just don't be someone who's minimizing their life by trying to "maximize" their high school, college, or early life experiences.

At every stage of your academic life, you will see people who are partying like there is no tomorrow. They never study, they rarely go to class, when they go to class they don't pay attention, and they are spending most of their time "maximizing" their fun in school. They "need" to be at every party, be in every picture, take every trip, be front row at every concert, and go to every event—put simply, they have a serious case of FOMO (fear of missing out). Don't be someone who lets FOMO destroy your life. These people oftentimes either flunk out of school or change their major to something that is easier but does not guarantee them any job prospects.

Post-graduation, when the people who had a bit less fun in college start their jobs, they can afford to take extravagant vacations and keep having fun. Whereas the people who "maximized" their fun in high school and/or college are now struggling to make ends meet. This the principle of delayed gratification at work.

And this principle doesn't just apply to academia, it also applies to life in general. In order to get to where we want to go, most of us have to take at least one intermediate job or train to acquire a specific skill set/certification. During the time you are working to acquire the necessary experience or skills to maximize your salary, you will have peers who are out having fun. While you are paying dues so that you can move up the ranks at your company or grow your own company, there will be concerts, events, and other exciting activities that you will miss.

And sometimes the thing you are delaying isn't just fun. For some of us, the thing that we are delaying is making the next career move in order to get specific experiences and credentials. Anybody who has been wildly successful has had at least one phase in their life where they had to endure the discomfort of paying dues. Whether it was taking the unpaid internship, hustling up low-paying gigs as opening acts, working multiple jobs, getting the difficult degree, or moving to a place you can't stand in order to take advantage of a great opportunity, we have all had to experience some temporary discomfort to achieve long-term success. By sacrificing a bit of comfort now to get degrees, experience, certifications, or credentials, you can attain greater success later.

> "I hated every minute of training, but I said, 'Don't quit. Suffer now and live the rest of your life as a CHAMPION.'"
> Muhammed Ali

However, when you are unwilling to delay gratification, you either accomplish less or each accomplishment costs you more. Think about our building metaphor. If you have ever had the great pleasure (or misfortune) of having to hire a contractor to do work on a building, you have likely seen the "Contractor Triangle." It is a triangle labeled with *Quality*, *Cost*, and *Time*. Typically, your contractor will use it as a tool to level-set your expectations about how long a job is going to take and/or how much it is going to cost. The idea is that you can have any two sides of the triangle, but you cannot have all three. This means that a job can be done at a high quality and a low price, but it will take a long time; a job can be done at a high quality and quickly, but it is going to be very expensive; or a job can be done quickly at a low cost, but it will be of low quality.

This same principle applies to building towards great accomplishments. In the context of your life, you can either choose to have *lower-quality achievements*, *sacrifice time*, or *pay a costly price* for attaining your goals. Take, for example, the goal of earning a large sum of money. If you adhere to the principle of delayed gratification, you take a bit longer to gather the education, training, connections, and experience needed to establish an extraordinarily lucrative career or a profitable business. By proactively working hard without taking shortcuts, it may take you a bit longer to start making significant money, but when you do, the large sum of money you make will be measured in hundreds of thousands or millions.

Conversely, what if you decide that you want to make the same amount of money but don't want to invest the time? The quality of your outcome is going to remain the same (i.e., you make the same amount of money), but you are going to take less time to get it. Using our Contractor Triangle, we know that means money will become more costly. What does that mean? How can money cost more? The first way in which money can cost more is your reputation. There are few things that you have that are innately valuable and irreplaceable once lost. Time is one of them; another is your reputation.

> "It takes 20 years to build a reputation and five minutes to ruin it. If you think about that, you'll do things differently."
> Warren Buffett

There are numerous unsavory manners to make money quickly: you can lie, cheat, steal, and do any number of things that devalue your worth as a human being. However, when you go down the path of chasing quick money in an unscrupulous manner, the cost to your reputation is something you can never recover. This doesn't just apply to making money—other examples include athletes who are caught cheating, people who plagiarize another's work, artists who knowingly put out low-quality work, and companies that knowingly sell unsafe products to increase short-term profitability. And what's the eventual outcome? Whether you call it lost goodwill, being disgraced, or simply disappointing your fans, it is all the same thing—you pay with your reputation when you chase quick unscrupulous shortcuts to success.

The other way in which money can cost more is that it can prevent you from making more money in the future. A perfect example of this is if attempting to make money quickly results in you doing something illegal. Once your actions are discovered and you are arrested and/or fired, you are going to find it hard to find a job in the future. Think of examples when a person's or organization's reputation is harmed. How many millions did the cyclists in those doping scandals lose? Look at Lance Armstrong in particular. A cheating scandal cost the famed cyclist millions in endorsement deals, lawsuits, and future revenue. What happened to the careers of singers after their lip-syncing scandals? What happens to hedge fund managers after a Ponzi scheme is discovered? In all of these cases, the person will get some quick money, but afterward, they risk having their money taken away and never being able to make money again.

The last possible configuration of the Contractor Triangle is accomplishments that are quick and inexpensive. These are the accomplishments you aim for when you are not very aggressive in setting lofty goals or pursuing big dreams. In the example of acquiring money, this would be making money in a way that doesn't take much time or harm your reputation. It is okay to set some goals that fall into this category. Practically speaking, not every one of your goals is going to be on the scale of Dr. King's dream. However, goals like this should be used to get you to bigger accomplishments. Examples might be needing a couple of hundred dollars to pay for books one semester or needing to save up enough to get a reliable car for your morning commute. As previously stated, the exercises and principles in this book can be applied to short-term goals as well as long-term dreams. Just make sure that all of your goals and dreams are not this type of short-term accomplishment.

Whether it is going to get more training before you enter the workforce, holding off on buying your dream car, or prioritizing addressing your needs so that you are able to better serve others, delayed gratification is an effective tool that will allow you to get more from life.

Note, however, that there is a difference between delayed gratification and just waiting. Delayed gratification is a combination of waiting and working. If you are not actively working, then you are just waiting for luck or serendipity, and that type of waiting is not an effective tool for success.

> "Being still and doing nothing are two completely different things."
> Jackie Chan

We have all heard the phrase "Good things come to those who wait." This phrase is basically saying that if you are patient, you can get greater rewards later on in life. Illustrating that point has been a major goal of this chapter. But waiting is only half the battle! Working is the necessary other half. Thus, I prefer the phrase "Good things come to those who wait, and *great* things come to those who *work!*"

Few people can say that a wonderful opportunity landed in their lap simply because they waited around for it. Generally, employers don't send unsolicited offer letters, investors don't write blank checks, and your soulmate doesn't come knocking on your door. If any of those things happen to you, then you are exceptionally blessed. However, for the rest of us, waiting isn't enough to make things happen.

Of course, there will be things you have to wait for in life. We will talk about the differences between requirements and suggestions in later chapters. However, there are some things that—as a matter of law—you must wait on. If your goal is to be President of the United States, you are constitutionally prohibited from accomplishing that goal in your 20s. If you want to be a cardiothoracic surgeon, you must wait and pass your board exams. And the list goes on.

However, waiting should not be your excuse to do nothing. You should be actively working to make sure that when the time comes, you are ready to seize your opportunities—acquire new skills, build your network, grow your knowledgebase, get healthier, and/or simply save money. Also, while patiently waiting on one goal, you can use your plan to identify other goals to progress towards. This type of active waiting is a form of multitasking we will discuss in later chapters.

And yes, patience and delayed gratification are necessary for success. But if you don't make sure to pair your patient waiting with persistent working, then you are never going to get all that you can from life. Don't be the person looking back with regret on your wasted time that you can never recover.

> "Good things come to those that wait.
> Great things come to those that work."

Chapter 9:
Celebrate EVERY Victory

Part of your planning process needs to include a reward system—this is a plan to celebrate your accomplishments both big and small. Why is this important? We talked a lot about motivation in previous chapters, and you should now know why you do the things you do and be heavily motivated by that rationale. However, sometimes it is hard to mentally make a direct connection between what you need to do on a daily or weekly basis and your overall motivations. In those moments, your reward system will give you the motivation you need to accomplish your daily, weekly, and monthly goals.

Let us use the example of preparing for a weekly meeting with a boss or advisor. To prepare for this meeting, you need to review material and prepare a presentation. However, bombing one meeting is unlikely to have a significant impact on accomplishing your dreams. As such, the big motivations that drive you to want to achieve your ambitions may fail you when preparing for your weekly meetings. Because you might have 25 to 50 of these meetings a year, being unprepared for or stumbling through one meeting is unlikely to derail your overall trajectory. So what is the big deal about one meeting?

It is true that, typically, messing up one weekly meeting, or one test, or one homework assignment will not have a long-term impact on your success. However, where do you draw the line? Thinking like this creates what we call a "slippery slope." If you intentionally miss one deadline, you might accidentally slip up and miss another, and another, and another. What happens when that one becomes two or three or a dozen? Eventually, you could slip up and actually cause long-term harm to your career or introduce unnecessary stumbling blocks into your journey.

Furthermore, what if that one meeting you didn't prepare for was the tipping point of a decision to promote? What if that one test or assignment was the difference between passing or failing, between keeping your scholarship or losing it? What if that one test meant meeting the GPA requirements for a job or missing out on an opportunity? You cannot account for all of the things that might go wrong in a given year. When you frivolously blow off assignments because you don't feel like doing them, you are consuming relationship capital. We will talk more about relationship capital later chapters, but every time someone gives you leniency or looks passed your laziness, you are consuming your relationship capital with that person. You don't want to need a big favor (e.g., leniency at the end of a semester, help in a major meeting, forgiveness for being unprepared, etc.), but have no relationship capital left to spend because you wasted it all haphazardly and unnecessarily.

Also, you never know when an unexpected opportunity will arise. What if you show up unprepared at the meeting and your advisor has invited someone they want you to impress? We are going to talk about how to effectively grow your team of mentors and sponsors in later chapters. However, one way to lose a valuable mentor or sponsor is to embarrass them in front of their peers. Before you walk into a room, you can never know what opportunities will be waiting on the other side of the door. Ultimately, you never know when you are going to get a golden opportunity to jump-start your dreams. Tyrese Gibson went from being a no-name model to an internationally known recording artist and actor because he gave his all singing in a Coca-Cola commercial.

> "If you stay ready, you don't have to get ready."
> Will Smith

I have given speeches in front of small audiences that have led to my most lucrative speaking engagements. I have had what I thought were casual meetings that quickly turned into job interviews. You always have to push yourself to be ready, because you never know when opportunity will knock. And you never know when the performance that nobody is supposed to see, the paper that nobody is supposed to read, or the project that nobody is supposed to care about will be the life-changing opportunity you have been waiting for.

Always being prepared is often easier said than done. How do you get past those times when you really don't feel like getting off of a full day of work or classes only to continue to work at home? How do you persevere in those moments when you *know* that slacking off "this one time" isn't going to be the end of the world? You cannot rely solely on knowing what drives you to get you through all of your day-to-day tasks. The solution that has worked for me in my personal, professional, and academic pursuits has been to set up a rewards system.

> "The more you praise and celebrate your life, the more there is in life to celebrate."
> Oprah Winfrey

A proper reward system ensures that every accomplishment —whether big or small—has a corresponding reward that you can look forward to. For example, I have always loved movies; probably because some of my earliest memories were going to the movie theater with my family. We would go to the dollar movie theater to see a few movies and then go across the street to an arcade. So, for me, seeing movies has always been something that I have found to be enjoyable, exciting, and relaxing. For that reason, I incorporated watching movies into my reward system in college. After every test I successfully studied for and completed, I would watch a movie. And after I completed a semester, I would get some of my favorite Rocky Road ice cream and have a movie marathon to celebrate.

This reward system worked for me in college because at 15 years old, those were some of my favorite things. However, my reward system in college is probably different than what yours will be. You must make your reward something you actually look forward to and enjoy. Whether it is eating at your favorite restaurant after successfully getting through your quarterly report, attending a party after mid-terms, or watching your favorite show after you successfully finished your weekly presentation, you should have something to look forward to after small victories.

Your reward system is something that is very personal for you and can consist of almost anything.

However, when setting up a reward system for yourself, there are three rules to follow: 1. *Celebrate the completion and not the result*, 2. *Make sure the celebration recharges you*, and 3. *Make sure the celebration is proportionate to the accomplishment.*

The first and most important rule of rewarding your victories is that your reward should not be contingent on the outcome. The victory is not the result—the victory is working your best to get through a task. Regardless of the result, you have achieved something just by working through your plan and hitting whatever milestone you have set for yourself.

Oftentimes, we feel like we are only deserving of a reward when we achieve the outcome we had hoped for. What we are really telling ourselves is that we are only worthy of a reward when someone else gives us approval. Thus, we do not reward ourselves unless we get a good grade or a promotion or win a competition. We tell ourselves that the judge, referee, teacher, opponent, or whoever else determines our outcome is the only person who can deem us worthy of appreciation. But that puts the source of your motivation in the hands of someone else, and you never want other people to have control over your psyche or to determine the value of your self-worth.

We have already discussed why motivations that are dependent on someone else are less effective. The same principle applies to your personal reward system. If the only time you reward yourself is when you receive the approval of someone else, then you are going to be less motivated to try when the outcome is uncertain. And even worse, if you are certain you *won't* get the approval you need, your reward system is rendered useless. There were times when I had to work tirelessly knowing that the likely outcome was going to be a form of failure.

Why work hard when you know you are probably going to fail? First and foremost, it is impossible to truly fail until you give up. Every unfavorable outcome that happens before you give up is just a temporary setback. You might not get to achieve some specific intermediate accomplishments, but you have never actually failed until you give up trying to accomplish your overall dreams.

Additionally, no matter how certain you are that you are "going to fail," you never truly know the outcome. And the only way that you are going to snatch victory from the jaws of near-certain defeat is by working to the best of your ability. Nobody beats the odds or wins stunning upsets with halfhearted attempts. Your reward system

> "Miracles only happen to those who never give up."
> Ivankov
> Emporio
> (*One Piece*)

should be designed to push you to put your all into it, even when circumstances seem bleak.

I remember one of the longest and most physically and mentally trying days of my life. I was working with a group on a medical device that could measure the heart and breathing rate of small infants. It was the night before a big presentation and our prototype was not working. Over the course of that night, my entire team disappeared one by one, leaving me alone to finish the design. I worked so long that I got to see the sunrise from my lab desk. However, when I left the lab, our prototype was fully functional and with ten hours to spare. I went home to get some much-deserved rest. Our mission was accomplished, and I was deserving of some rest before our presentation that afternoon.

Within a couple of hours of when my head hit my pillow, my phone began to ring continually. In the hours since I had completed and tested our fully functioning device, one of my group members had the *bright idea* that the circuit I built was not "pretty enough"—in case you were wondering, "pretty" was not one of the design criteria for this class. Nevertheless, my groupmate removed all of the wires I had painstakingly put together to form a complex network of circuits, made them "prettier," and then tried to put them back together.

I am sure you can see where this is going. They could not reconstruct my circuit. With less than seven hours to go until the demonstration and less than three hours of sleep, I had to find a way to do what had initially taken me three days to figure out. I committed to myself that I was going to work tirelessly for the entire seven hours and that regardless of how horribly it turned out, I was going to take a long, coma-like nap with no phone nearby, and then I was going to watch multiple movies and get some Rocky Road ice cream.

The mental, physical, and emotional fatigue of this ordeal started to seriously take its toll. This was compounded when my groupmates left me by myself in the lab again. Eventually, I started bargaining with myself, thinking things like, "Maybe bombing this demonstration wouldn't get me too far off track from my goals. It is just one demonstration in a year-long project." When those thoughts crept into my mind, I reminded myself about my reward system. If I didn't work through all seven hours, then I wouldn't get the rewards I had promised myself.

Of course, it was impossible for me to duplicate what I had built over the course of several days in a few drowsy hours. However, because I kept working, I figured out a shortcut and managed to repair the prototype and enable it to perform just well enough to get through the demonstration. Although it wasn't up to the standard I would have liked, it was more than enough to get the approval for the next phase of its design.

In this circumstance, I was going to get my reward regardless of how things turned out, but only if I worked hard for the entire time. Because I was motivated to work hard, I was pleasantly surprised by the outcome. Still, even if my fears had been realized and the demonstration had turned out to be less than successful, I would have given myself the same rewards. Because of that fact, I diligently kept working and managed to snatch victory from near-certain failure. Situations like this are the reason why your rewards system *must* be based on your effort/completion and not based on the outcome.

Along with being contingent on completion instead of outcome, your reward system must actually make you feel recharged. Much like your motivation, it has to be personal to you. In my experience, something recharges you when it *legitimately lifts your spirits* AND *appropriately refreshes you*. That "and" is important. Your reward system is something that is supposed to push you to be continually prepared to work at a high level. Each reward must be like a springboard, launching you into the next task by lifting your spirits and refreshing you.

The concept of lifting your spirits is pretty self-explanatory: a reward should be something that makes you happier, more joyous, and/or fills you with laughter and excitement. However, what does it mean to be appropriately refreshed? Being appropriately refreshed means having your mental, physical, and/or emotional energy restored with enough time to begin your next task. A reward is not *appropriately* refreshing if it stops you from being ready to complete the rest of your work. Thus, the type of reward you give yourself will change based on how much time you have before needing to resume work. If this task is the last thing you have to do before taking an extended vacation, then almost anything you like doing can be appropriately refreshing. However, if you have to do your next task the next day, then you have to be more selective about your reward.

Let's say you are somebody who loves to play basketball—thus, it lifts your spirits. But for some of the more "seasoned" readers, your recovery time might not be the same as it used to be. If every time you play basketball, you end up needing to sit in Epson salt and are bedridden for a day, be careful how you incorporate basketball into your reward system. When your next task is within a day or two of your last task, playing basketball is not something that would be considered appropriately refreshing. Thus, unless you have an extended delay before your next task, playing basketball would not be a good reward.

Conversely, if you are somebody who loves sweets, ice cream might be very refreshing for you. However, if you are also on a diet and are going to feel guilty about eating ice cream, then it isn't something that is going to lift your spirits. As such, ice cream probably wouldn't be a good reward for you.

Note that it is okay if you do not take your reward on the same day you earn it. If you have back-to-back tests or are working on a project that includes multiple parts, you may want to wait until you have completed everything to partake in your reward for your hard work. Just be careful that you are actually engaged in delayed gratification and not just depriving yourself of something you have earned. (Remember our "Delayed Gratification" chapter!)

In situations where you cannot partake in your reward immediately, I strongly encourage you to keep a tally of everything you owe yourself so that you don't forget. Also, have a quick, refreshing reward you can give yourself now.

Your reward can be anything you choose. You can go to a party, buy yourself a gift, go out to eat, cook yourself something special, or take a trip. It can be as simple as getting yourself a Twinkie or as big as going to see your favorite artist in concert. You can have it be something you do solo, or if you are a social person, it can be meeting up with some friends you haven't seen in a while. As long as your reward lifts your spirits and appropriately refreshes you, it is completely up to you.

> "Zombieland Rule #32: Enjoy the little things."

However, one caveat is that your reward should not be a necessity. In cases where you are rewarding yourself with a necessity, you have developed a punishment system and not a reward system. What does that mean? If your reward to yourself is anything that falls within Maslow's Hierarchy of Physiological or Safety Needs (food, water, shelter, etc.), you are not rewarding yourself for completing a task—instead, you are punishing yourself if you do *not* complete your task. In other words, your reward to yourself should never be the avoidance of harm to yourself, because that is a system that relies on punishment, which is not as effective.

What are examples of punishment systems? There are extreme versions of punishment-based systems, like "If I finish this book tonight, I won't make myself run bleachers tomorrow" or "If I finish this report, I won't flog myself." I would pray you would not do that to yourself. You also have to be careful about more subtle versions of punishment systems, like, "If I finish studying this, then I will let myself go to sleep" or "When I get through this presentation without stumbling, I will go get dinner." In reality, you are not rewarding yourself—you are saying that if you fail, you don't get to sleep or eat respectively.

Compare this to a true reward system: "If I finish studying this, then I will let myself sleep in for an *extra* two hours" or "When I get through this presentation without stumbling, I will get a cupcake to go with my dinner." Reward systems are about giving yourself something extra you wouldn't normally receive.

The reason you don't want to set up a punishment-based system for yourself is that it is *harder to maintain* and *can make you resentful*. Punishment-based systems only work when the person giving the punishment is not the same person receiving it. In order for this short-term motivation system to work, you have to have consistency. If the person implementing your punishment is yourself, you are inevitably going to give yourself mercy. Thus, you will not consistently follow through with your threats, and the motivation factor reduces.

On the off chance that you are consistent with your punishments, you are going to become resentful. Whenever you are being punished, you resent your punisher; that is human nature. Think about how often we hear of people threatening their judge or prosecutor in a criminal case. In this case, you are the one punishing yourself. Even worse, you are creating a mental correlation between the accomplishment of your dream and being punished. It will not be long until you associate the pain of your punishment with your dream and resent the dream itself.

We have seen this play out with several entertainers and athletes who were pushed incredibly hard by punishment-based systems—their parents, advisors, and/or coaches punished them harshly for their shortcomings or mistakes. Ultimately, they ended up resenting their careers, their punishers, and themselves. That resentment perverted their dream into a source of anguish and spite. When that happened, their dreams morphed from something they loved and pursued into something they hated and ran from.

For these reasons, reward systems are far more effective tools than punishment systems for driving you to long-term success and happiness. So make sure your reward system is actually a reward system and not a punishment system in disguise.

The last requirement of a reward system is that it be proportional to the accomplishment. This has been implied throughout this chapter, but I wanted to make it unequivocally clear: do not be somebody who rewards yourself with a TV show for every page you read. Your reward system is not a license to perpetually indulge in distractions. The reward should correspond to completing a legitimate and significant task or a major milestone. If you want your reward to be a 30-minute TV show, make that be the reward for reading an entire chapter. Or if you want to be rewarded per page, make the reward be one of your favorite chips and eat a Dorito every time you turn a page. But the work should take significantly longer than the reward.

For some people, their issue is using a reward system as an excuse to indulge in distractions; others have the exact opposite problem. For example, your reward for completing a four-year journey should not be a cupcake. (After every one of my graduations, I celebrated with a party and a trip to somewhere.) Understand that celebrating your milestones is a necessary part of achieving success and should be done even when it isn't convenient.

The week after I graduated from law school, I had to start studying for the bar exam for three months, and the week after finishing the bar exam, I started my PhD program. I had no time to properly celebrate this milestone, so I was creative with finding time for my trip and my party. Since I wasn't going to have time for a trip after graduation, I took it *before* graduation—the day after finishing finals, I flew to Los Angeles to see one of my favorite artists in concert. Then I waited until a month into my PhD program to celebrate with my family and friends. I did not allow the time constraint to be an excuse not to properly reward myself for the lengthy and difficult journey of successfully completing law school. Remember, delayed gratification is an effective tool for maximizing your time.

> "Life ain't no dress rehearsal."
> Bernie Mac

If you don't make time to celebrate your big and small victories with appropriate rewards, you will burn out before you reach your dream. So many people think success means working endlessly.

Yes, hard work is a necessity to succeed in life, but rest, relaxation, and fun are necessities, too! Although my almost-two-decades-long journey has been challenging, I have found ways to have fun at every stage of it.

The fun times are not just frivolous indulgences. I have seen many people lie and pretend that the secret to success is never taking a break, but I have never seen someone attain and maintain long-term success without having fun and celebrating along the way. Fun reenergizes you for the difficult segments of your journey. As such, it is important to find ways to enjoy the journey towards your dream. Use your reward system as a way to ensure that you find joy in your journey and not just obligations and stress.

Once you have developed your reward system, make sure to periodically update it. Your reward system should remain proportionate to your effort. The more you do things, the better you get at them and the more effortless they become. Maybe the first few months of having to prepare a weekly report were difficult for you, but now it takes you less than 20 minutes to complete it. Or maybe it used to take you days to type a paper, but now it's something you can do in a few hours. You must update the reward criteria to reflect your new ability. Maybe you give yourself the same reward for completing a month's worth of the weekly reports that you used to give yourself weekly. Or maybe you find a new challenge to reward yourself weekly for doing. Regardless of how you approach it, you always want to ensure that your reward system remains appropriately proportional to your effort.

Also, update your rewards as your tastes change. As I have mentioned before, I used to love Rocky Road ice cream. As such, I incorporated it heavily into my reward system. However, as I got older, my taste buds changed. I still love Rocky Road ice cream, but now my sweet tooth just isn't as strong as it used to be, and the idea of eating a pint of ice cream seems more like a chore than a reward. As such, a good steak has replaced Rocky Road ice cream as my go-to reward for a hard week.

As your tastes change, your rewards should change with them. This does not just apply to food, this rule also applies to activities. Maybe going to bars and parties is not as refreshing and uplifting for you as it used to be. You might also have found activities you didn't even know you liked. For example, some of my friends from other states have been surprised to find out how much they enjoy going to gun ranges. Target shooting went from something they had never tried to something they thoroughly enjoyed doing. Similarly, some of my friends who ran track in high school and college went from loving to run to having done it so much they now hate it. We all go through different phases of our life where we enjoy different things. Therefore, periodically reevaluate the activities that comprise your reward system.

The objective of establishing a system for rewarding your victories (both big and small) is to drive you to fully apply yourself to short-term goals. Your reward system can incentivize you to work hard in situations where your core motivation may not be a sufficient driving force. And if it is properly established, appropriately updated, and consistently implemented, your reward system will drive you to consistently be prepared and excel on a daily basis.

"Constant effort is life's greatest shortcut."
Kamogawa Genji
(*Hajime no Ippo*)

Chapter 10:
Work Smart

Throughout this book, we have talked about working hard. Now let's talk about working smart.

If you ran as hard and fast as you could, how long would it take you to run to a town one mile away? It could take minutes, hours, years, a lifetime, or forever, depending on the route you take. Sure, if you choose the most direct route and run in a straight line, you'd probably make it to the next town in 10 to 30 minutes. But what if you ran in zigzags or circles? What if instead of running directly to the town, you ran in the opposite direction and attempted to circumnavigate the globe? Or what if you spent the entire time running on a treadmill? You could literally run hundreds or even thousands of miles but would never get anywhere.

In all of these contexts, you are working hard (i.e., running your fastest). So if you are working hard in all of these examples, why would some examples of reaching your destination take minutes and others take years? The difference lies in how smart you are in choosing how to apply your energy.

As our example demonstrates, hard work is not a guarantee of success or even progress—some people work hard on a daily basis without progressing towards a goal. However, anyone who pairs working hard with working smart has a sure recipe for success.

> "We must use time creatively, in the knowledge that the time is always ripe to do right."
> Dr. Martin Luther King, Jr.

The first method for working smart that I want to introduce is the concept of multitasking. We have largely talked about pursuing goals as if it is always a linear process. Each step has had one step that precedes it, and you can only do one thing at a time. To some extent, there will be parts of your journey that will proceed in this kind of linear fashion. However, most of the time, you will have the option to multitask on some level. Effective use of multitasking can greatly increase the speed at which you progress towards your dream.

When I say "multitasking," it may conjure a cartoonish image of a person doing a different task with each hand simultaneously. However, multitasking in this context does not necessarily mean doing multiple things simultaneously. Trying to do multiple complex activities at the same time is an impractical approach to most multitasking. In this context, a more accurate view of multitasking is beginning or resuming a new task before the current task is complete.

An example of multitasking in an industrial context is a team drilling for oil in a difficult area. When you are drilling deep or through earth that is hard or inconsistent, a lot of possible problems can arise. One of those problems is that your drill bit may unexpectedly break underground. When this happens, you need a new drill bit. If the cause of the break was the unexpected characteristics of the ground you are drilling in, you may need a new type of drill bit.

Depending on how rare this part is or if it needs to be custom-fabricated, getting a new drill bit can take several days. During that time, dozens of members of the drill team can no longer drill for oil. While waiting for the new part to arrive, will those employees be sitting on their hands? No! Time is money, and the team is going to try to maximize their time so that they maximize their profits. An efficient drill team will perform diagnostic checks to ensure that nothing else breaks when drilling resumes, prepare the rig to install the new drill bit, and may even get a head start on routine maintenance of the equipment. By doing so, they reduce the total time it will take for them to complete the project and reach their goal. This method of multitasking is something we often do at work but are sometimes less willing to apply to our personal life.

If we treated our personal life like we do our work projects, whenever we had downtime in one area of our lives, we would work towards progress in another area. This type of active waiting is a concept we have discussed multiple times in previous chapters. One of the reasons we start by developing a comprehensive plan, is so we are better able to identify multitasking opportunities.

Consider the example of wanting to start a business. If you were effectively multitasking, when you had lulls in your life, you would actively pursue growing your business. This means that whenever you had additional time, you would perform tasks that would get you closer to owning a business.

Unfortunately, this is not the way most of us approach achieving our goals. Oftentimes, we will only work on one thing at a time. Rather than continuously working towards starting a business, we start by dedicating ourselves to school. Then, once we've completed school, we dedicate ourselves to getting more work experience. Then, once we have gotten more work experience, we start the background research to figure out our plan for starting a business. But working this way instead of multitasking will result in you taking much longer to get to your destination…if you get there at all.

What you are doing in this context is creating false prerequisites to achieving your goal. Multitasking is a useful tool, but in order to properly multitask, you have to have a clear vision of the complete plan. This is why creating a plan is such an important part of the process.

Let's return to our building analogy. By having a framework established (e.g., a total list of goals) and a complete blueprint (e.g., your plan), you can build towards your dream more efficiently. Think about constructing a house. How do the builders progress through the project? Do they build each room to completion and then move on to the next room? No. Builders have phases of the project and complete each phase for the entire home. One day may be inserting insulation, one afternoon may be putting in drywall, one evening may be putting in carpet and so on. Additionally, builders have multiple different tasks going on simultaneously in different rooms of the house. (Thus, a plumber and electrician may be onsite at the same time.) In this manner, builders proceed through each phase until the construction project is complete.

The reason that builders are able to do this is because the frame of the house lets them know where everything is going to be and the blueprint gives them a view of the steps necessary to finish the project. This allows them to progress towards completion more quickly by multitasking and working on multiple areas of the structure simultaneously.

How would this work practically? If your dream is to own an automotive repair shop, you would need to learn about business ownership and cars. In order to get that base level of knowledge, you could work to become an expert in cars and then go back to school to become an expert in all things business. But that would be the equivalent of completing construction on one room before beginning construction on the next. A more efficient way of doing things would be to work towards becoming an expert in auto repair while simultaneously taking supplemental classes or reviewing supplemental material to learn about business.

Multitasking is not always an option—sometimes, some things must be completed before others (i.e., prerequisite tasks). Part of the reason it is important to realize that multitasking is possible is so that you actually take the time to learn what the prerequisite tasks are to achieving your goals. Quite often, we assume what the prerequisite tasks are, but we never actually take the time to test their necessity. Thus, we end up putting up artificial roadblocks to our success.

> "We must open the doors of opportunity. But we must also equip our people to walk through those doors."
> Pres. Lyndon B. Johnson

When mentoring young professionals, this is oftentimes the most difficult lesson to teach. I cannot tell you how many times I have heard "But what I really want to do is X." That "X" could be starting a business, changing a career, moving into a new division, moving into a leadership position, or any number of other aspirations.

Invariably, whenever I ask, "Well, why wait?" the answer is always that they feel they need to get more experience, an additional degree, or an intermediate position. In their minds, they have established all of these required prerequisites to where they want to be in life, yet most of them are not actually real.

> "We have to build things we want to see accomplished, in life and in our country..."
> Rep. Patsy Matsu Takemoto Mink

A required prerequisite is something that is required by a written regulation, law, or policy, or a law of nature. If there is not an unbreakable rule or a law that explicitly tells you something is a prerequisite to one of your goals or your dream, you are not required to complete it before proceeding to the next step. I want you to really internalize that statement. *Unless there is a law or an unbreakable rule that tells you that you are required to do it before undertaking your goal or dream, you may multitask.* The reason I reiterate this point is because most of us put artificial prerequisites on ourselves.

Here is an example of this principle: there is a law in each state of the United States that prevents you from practicing law without being properly licensed by a licensing board. These boards require the completion of a law degree before you can receive your license. This is a rule that the licensing boards do not make exceptions for. The schools that issue these degrees strongly recommend that their students work at least a year or two before applying for admissions. Based on what I have told you, what are the prerequisites to practicing law in the U.S.A.?

Working for at least a year before getting a law degree and then becoming licensed, right? Although I agree that getting a law degree and becoming licensed are prerequisites, nothing actually requires you to work for a year. A lot of us hear phrases like "we strongly recommend," "we encourage," "we strongly discourage," "you should," and "it would be best if you…" and interpret them as "you must." That is not the case.

I have spent the majority of my life taking on challenges that I was "strongly recommended" to avoid. It was strongly recommended that I not start the third grade at six years old. I was strongly discouraged from taking such a heavy course load during my

> *"All I got is dreams. Nobody else believes. Nobody else can see. Nobody else but me."*
> Shawn "Jay-Z" Carter

first year in college. I only made two B's that year; the rest of my grades were straight A's. When I was applying to law school, my pre-law advisor flat-out told me to set my sights lower because he didn't believe that I was a strong enough candidate to get into a Top 20-ranked law school. I ignored that recommendation and got admitted to and graduated from Harvard Law School. Most recently, I was strongly discouraged from taking such a rigorous PhD curriculum. If I hadn't taken the time to clearly understand the difference between requirements and suggestions, I would have never reached the goal of graduating with my three degrees before the age of 26.

If you are doing anything remotely ambitious or working on a timeline that is aggressive, you are going to have people try to slow you down with "encouragement" and "discouragement":

> *"I encourage you to get a bit more work experience."*
> *"I discourage you from pursuing that career."*
> *"You should consider something less risky."*
> *"You should think about how that will look."*
> *"I think it would be best for you to get more education before you start."*

And the list will go on and on.

Multitasking can be a challenge, but you are the only one who knows the type of workload you can handle. Don't allow people to cause you to second-guess your ability. If you know you have the time and talent to pursue multiple goals simultaneously, pursue them!

I am not suggesting for you to ignore wise counsel when it is given. I am, however, saying that not all counsel given is wise. In my various situations, none of the people offering me their "strong recommendations" and unsolicited advice were part of my team. Therefore, they had little understanding of my capabilities and no real understanding of my journey to that point. When confronted with a suggestion or recommendation that contradicted my trajectory, I would always consult my team. If my team agreed with the suggestion, I would add it in as an intermediary step. However, I would do so knowing that it was a choice that I could revisit if necessary. Just because everyone around me suggested something did not make it a requirement. There were times that I even went against the suggestions of my close advisors and mentors.

> "We're all human at the end of the day, making mistakes. But learning from them is key."
> Kendrick Lamar

Knowing who is part of your team and whose advice to take is something we will address in later chapters. We are also going to talk in greater detail about when it is necessary to act against the advice of trusted team members. However, I want to note that it is never acceptable to ignore the advice of somebody you consider part of your team (e.g., a coach, mentor, sponsor, advisor, etc.). You should consider what they are telling you, address the concerns they raise using the fear versus apprehension and risk mitigation techniques discussed in earlier chapters, and make an informed decision after considering all of the facts. Remember, it is okay to agree to disagree, but it is never okay to ignore a well-intentioned voice of reason.

———————

In addition to effective multitasking, another method for working smart is to know the Point of Diminishing Returns and not go beyond it. Typically, regardless of what you are working on, there is a strong and positive correlation between the time you spend on something and an improved outcome. If you spend an extra 30 minutes on a presentation, then you are typically going to improve the quality of that presentation. Similarly, if you spend an extra hour studying, you can reasonably expect to see an improvement in your grade. If you spend an extra day on product development, you are typically going to see a proportionate increase in product quality. All of this is typically true…except when you have gone beyond the Point of Diminishing Returns.

What is the Point of Diminishing Returns? It is a point at which working additional hours starts having less impact on your outcome. Another way of looking at it is that the Point of Diminishing Returns is the point where— after extensive work on a project or assignment has been performed—the amount of time and effort you will have to put in to improve the results ceases to be possible or reasonable.

Think about taking a test back in high school. The amount of effort you had to put in to go from a score of 0% to a score of 50% might have been an hour, and to go from 50% to 70% might have taken another hour. Maybe with another hour of studying, your grade would have increased from 70% to 93%. However, if you wanted to get a perfect score on the test, then you would have had to have known every obscure reference the teacher might have chosen from the material. So instead of taking another hour to get that perfect score, it took you an additional two hours to get from 93% to that perfect score of 100%. Was it worth it to almost double your study time to raise your grade from an A to a higher A? In most cases, the answer is no. Thus, the three-hour mark that got you to a 93% was your Point of Diminishing Returns. The amount of studying you will have to do to improve your grade passed this point is unreasonable when compared with the outcome.

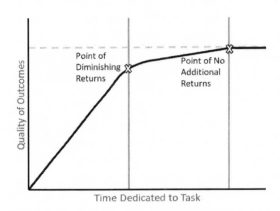

Closely related to the Point of Diminishing Returns is the Point of No Additional Returns. When you have gone so far beyond the Point of Diminishing Returns that you have gotten as close to perfect as you can possibly get, this is when you hit the Point of No Additional Returns. This means that no matter how much more time and effort you put into a particular task, you will never increase the quality of your outcome. This is when people say that you are "spinning your wheels."

In the previous example of taking a test, the Point of No Additional Returns would occur after you have studied the material for five hours and are going to get a perfect or near-perfect score. Studying the material for another hour or two would do nothing to improve your grade.

In general, a telltale sign that you have hit the point of No Additional Returns is when you find yourself engaged in a repetitive loop. An example could be repeated oscillating between two equally good decisions. Let's say you are working on a presentation and you keep going back and forth between two font selections for the title slide. Both fonts work functionally, but you keep going back and forth on which one is most aesthetically pleasing. If you are working on such trivial minutia, you have likely passed the Point of No Additional Returns. Whenever you realize that you have passed the Point of No Additional Returns, you should definitely start working on other tasks.

Now, there are times you might work past the Point of Diminishing Returns because you need to be as perfect as possible for a given assignment, but there is never a reason to work beyond the Point of No Additional Returns. Being able to identify these points is an effective way of allocating your time and effort to work smart and maximize your overall success.

This premise is especially true if you are juggling multiple assignments at the same time. Using the test example, let's say that all tests operated according to this same grade-to-study-time correlation. In the time it takes a student to study to get a perfect score in two exams, that student could have finished studying to get an A on three exams. Keep in mind that studying for the perfect scores would not actually improve their GPA and could in fact hurt their GPA if they ran out of time while trying to study for their third exam. Thus, in this scenario, trying to study to get from 93% to 100% is an example of reaching (and exceeding) the Point of Diminishing Returns.

This same principle applies to everything you do. Perfectionists are not the successful people in this world. The people who are most successful are the ones who realize that perfection is a pipe dream and that consistent high quality is their standard. If you allow perfect to be the enemy of great and great to be the enemy of good, you will consistently be playing catch-up and will never have enough time to achieve your maximum capability.

> "Love the life you live. Live the life you love."
> Bob Marley

Note, however, that there are some things in life with no margin for error. If you are a brain surgeon or a nuclear physicist, doing your job at only an A-level can cost people their lives. Still, knowing your Point of Diminishing Returns can still be helpful to create more time to do the things you need to be perfect at. For example, if you are a nuclear physicist, you do not need to waste time preparing your daily coffee with the same precision you employ when conducting fission reactions. The purpose of identifying the Point of Diminishing Returns then becomes to reduce the amount of time you spend on activities with lower importance. This allows you to have more time to dedicate to major tasks.

When you are pursuing lofty goals, time will often be a resource you wish you had more of. Fortunately, you have been blessed with the same 24-hour day as everyone else. Working smart with universal time constraints directly impacts our ability to achieve our goals. Since there is no way to make days longer, the best way to gain more time is to most efficiently use the time you have. For me, effective multitasking and knowing the Point of Diminishing Returns (and the Point of No Additional Returns) has consistently allowed me to do more with seemingly less available time.

Chapter 11:
Finish What You Start

When I travel to high schools and universities around the country to speak, I pretty consistently ask one question: "What is the one thing you can get from a college that you can't get anywhere else?"

Typically, students will respond with things like "life experiences," "lifelong friendships," or "an education." All of those answers are wrong. Even without going to college, you can have plenty of the same life experiences. I have met a good number of my lifelong friends in high school and through work. Additionally, with the availability of books and internet resources, you can surely get an education outside of college. The truth is, with the exception of one thing, all of what you get in college you can get somewhere else.

Eventually, if nobody guesses it, I will let them know the answer: "A college degree!" A college degree is the only thing you can get from college that you cannot get anywhere else. The point of this exercise is to show them something that I am hoping to show you: *There is a lot of value in finishing what you start.*

I recognize that a vast number of my readers are not high school or college students. Nevertheless, I began this chapter with the example of college because it perfectly illustrates the message of this chapter. You derive the most value from college when you finish it! At most companies, there is *not* a substantial difference between the pay of a full-time employee who has "some college" over that of a full-time employee who only has a high school diploma. And if the person with a high school diploma has completed any certifications, they will get paid more than the person who started college and did not finish. Thus, if you go to college for the experience and without a plan to graduate with a worthwhile degree, then you are not capturing the value of college. Furthermore, you are likely going to be putting yourself in a worse position, because you will have paid the cost of college without deriving its primary benefit (i.e., a college degree).

This is a reminder that the purpose of setting goals and working towards them is to finish them. In the words of Brandy Norwood, "Almost doesn't count." That applies here as well. Almost accomplishing your goals or almost making your dream come true is not the purpose of this book. When utilizing this information, the objective is to complete all of your goals and achieve your dream.

Using the college example, we are going to examine some of the reasons why people don't finish what they start. Although we are using the running example of college, these same reasons apply to any goal or dream people start but do not complete. The top reasons I have seen for people not finishing college are: 1. *No motivation*, 2. *No planning*, 3. *No delayed gratification*, and 4. *No interim checkpoints*. At this point in the book, you have the tools to overcome all of these pitfalls.

A reoccurring theme in this book is that you will not achieve a long-term goal that is not solidly grounded in your core motivations. A lack of motivation creates a lack of consistency and follow-through. When your actions are tied to something that drives you, you are more likely to put in consistent effort. As such, all of your goals and dreams should be firmly grounded in one or more of your core motivations. When you do this, your motivation will make you feel uneasy and bothered if you ever get off track from your goals.

> "Without commitment, you'll never start. But without consistency, you'll never finish."
> Denzel Washington

I am sure you have heard the phrase "It's a marathon and not a sprint" when referring to achieving long-term goals. That is a good analogy for discussing motivation. Anyone who has trained for or ran a marathon has hit something they call "the wall." This is a point in the race where it literally feels like you cannot move another step because of your mental and physical exhaustion. It almost feels like a wall is standing in front of you.

When "running the marathon" of pursuing long-term goals, we all hit that same wall at some point. It is the point where the siren call of quitting echoes in your head, and you think, "It wouldn't be so bad—I've already accomplished quite a bit." When people who are not properly motivated hit this wall, they yield to the temptation of quitting.

For me, I hit a major "wall" as I was exiting law school. A Harvard attorney working at a major law firm doing transactional and IP law makes more money in a year than I had made in my lifetime. I was looking at the combination of benefits, perks, mandatory annual pay raises, and bonuses stacked on top of a ridiculous base salary, and I was forced to ask myself, "Why are you considering getting another degree?"

> "To make a great dream come true, the first requirement is a great capacity to dream; the second is persistence."
> Cesar Chavez

If, at that moment, I had not had a clear picture of why I was pursuing a PhD, what I expected to accomplish, and why going straight into a law firm was a detour from my long-term desires for my professional and personal life, I would have given up. However, my core motivations still remained: to be able to provide for and support my family. And even though my pay would have been substantial, it wouldn't have been the level I needed to be able to fulfill that aspiration. Additionally, the time commitment would have prevented me from being there when people needed me. Because of my core motivations, I was able to resist the temptation to quit and instead keep racing towards my dreams.

There have been other times that I have hit a wall and wanted to quit. At each of those junctures, the pain of quitting exceeded the discomfort of continuing because I was properly motivated. However, I chose this example to illustrate a point. Sometimes the temptation you are fighting is objectively a good one—in my instance, having a high-paying job as an attorney would have been a wonderful thing. I had numerous people feel (and tell me) that I was making a mistake by continuing to pursue my dreams. You might experience the same thing, but remember, you are the only one who has to see and believe in your vision to make it a reality. Now that the people around me are beginning to see the end results of my pursuit, nobody questions whether I made the correct decision.

The second reason I have seen people fail to complete college was because they did not have an established plan for success. "If you fail to plan, you plan to fail," as the saying goes. A person who doesn't have a clearly articulated plan for success has basically created a plan for failure. Generally, if you are pursuing something extraordinary, there are many more ways to fail than there are to succeed. Thus, if you haphazardly stumble towards a dream without a plan, you are far more likely to go down a path of failure rather than a path to success. Creating a plan ensures that you are going in the correct direction.

Remember that your plan should also include a planned reward system, because your reward system helps you stay driven when your core motivations are not enough. Also, your plan will never be perfect, so once you have a workable plan, start building towards your dream. While working to accomplish your goals, you should update your plan to reflect changing circumstances, newly available shortcuts, and new information. Remember, as long as you are working your plan, you can avoid being distracted or derailed by detours.

The next major pitfall is the inability to utilize delayed gratification. Delayed gratification is a tool that allows you to achieve and gain more while also allowing your achievements to cost you less. By being patient and engaging in active waiting, you are able to accomplish more and have greater long-term success. If you are in a perpetual state of instant gratification, you are unable to properly invest in your future! Pursuing your dreams is an investment of time, money, and energy into creating a better future. If you are unwilling to make that investment, you will have all of your benefits now and spend the rest of your life paying for them.

Typically, the people who don't finish college are realizing the short-term benefits of fun and reduced stress. However, in order to pay for those short-term benefits, they are giving up the future opportunities their college degree would have afforded them. If you are unwilling to sacrifice a bit of comfort now, you will be forced to live with the discomfort of having given up for the rest of your life, whereas with delayed gratification, you invest a bit of up-front work and reap the benefits of it for years to come.

Finally, as previously discussed, it is important to establish intermediate milestones and to celebrate when you successfully complete those milestones. A lot of the time, people quit because they cannot see the "light at the end of the tunnel." Attaining that last degree seems so far off and distant that you feel like you will never make it. The more ambitious and longer-term your dream is, the more difficult it will be to maintain motivation throughout your journey.

To combat this, we talked about establishing milestone victories that you can celebrate along the way to making your dream a reality. You must break up your larger journey into more digestible portions that you can wrap your mind around. This is a method for sustaining your motivation over longer periods of time.

The other benefit of establishing intermediate goals is that it helps you combat procrastination. In my experience, most people (myself included!) have a tendency to procrastinate. We wait until we need to do something or we are close to the deadline to complete a task even if we started well in advance. This tendency towards procrastination can derail long-term accomplishments. In contrast, having intermediate goals helps combat the negative impact of the tendency to procrastinate. Even if you procrastinate on each individual intermediate goal, you will be making continuous progress towards your overall goal. In this way, having intermediate goals helps you pace your progress and combats procrastination.

The tools I just mentioned—along with the other information included in this book—address what I have seen to be some of the largest barriers to success. However, no matter how many tools I give you, it is you who must decide to use them. I speak from personal experience when I say that if you apply these principles, you can make your dreams come true. Nevertheless, this only works if you commit to pursuing your passions and never give up on your dreams. Commit to yourself that once you start this journey, you will not give up until you finish!

> "Strength does not come from physical capacity. It comes from an indomitable will."
> Mahatma Gandhi

Chapter 12:
Get the Right Team

You can achieve success through a good plan, hard work, determination, and follow-through. However, if you want to maximize your success, it requires a team effort. Everyone who wants to do something extraordinary in life should have a solid team. This is your inner circle of people who help keep you on track to achieving your dreams. There are a lot of team members and types of team members you can have, but I believe that every team needs a coach, a mentor, a sponsor, and a cheerleader, and you need to know the difference between each of them.

- Coaches -

Your coach is a person who knows you the best and can provide you with candid advice about how to conduct yourself. This person is the sounding board you can be most open with and with whom you can air out all of your "dirty laundry." They know your vices, your shortcomings, and your history, so there is never a need to put on a front when you are around your coach.

Much like an athlete has multiple coaches for different situations and stages of their career, you will have multiple coaches, too. All of my real friends are also my coaches. Still, none of them are able to coach me in *every* aspect of my life. For example, the person I go to for dating advice isn't the same person I go to for advice on dealing with my boss.

Know your coaches' limitations. Floyd Mayweather, Jr. wouldn't get a coach who has never worn boxing gloves to train him for a fight. Similarly, you should not get a coach who has never held a job to give you work-related advice. Nor should you allow your most short-tempered and confrontational friend to give you advice on de-escalating a conflict. Know what each of your coaches' strengths and weaknesses are and utilize them accordingly.

This is a good time to point out that if you don't have friends who can coach you on some aspect of your life, you should probably get new friends. Back home, we have a saying: "Don't be the biggest fish in a little pond." Yes, it can be a comfortable feeling to be better than all of your friends at everything (i.e., being the biggest fish). These are situations where you are always the best on your team, you always know you are going to win, and/or everyone always defers to you. However, remember our discussion about discomfort. You have to leave your comfort zone to maximize your growth. Having nobody to challenge you means you have nobody who can push you to grow. Though it is comfortable to be around people you always know more than or are better than, you will slow your progression towards your goals and stunt your personal growth.

Also understand that in this scenario, even though *you* are being lulled into complacency, everyone around you is being motivated to improve. Some of you have already seen that a lot of the people who were naturally talented early on in life ended up leading mediocre lives; whereas the people who struggled early to catch up to their naturally talented peers learned the work ethic and drive that kept them progressing towards success.

Look at Michael Jordan—not making the varsity team in his sophomore year of high school in 1978 was something that motivated him for the next 25 years of his basketball career. Having a few older kids in high school who were better than him gave him drive to continuously progress even after he became better than any of those kids could ever hope to be.

Don't be the biggest fish in a little pond. You will end up unilaterally motivating the people around you while becoming stagnant yourself. Instead, always seek the discomfort of growth. Surround yourself with talented people who can challenge you to improve. Any person whom I call "friend" is or *has been* better than me at something. As such, there is some aspect of my spiritual, personal, or professional development that they can guide me through. If someone does not possess that ability, then it is difficult for me to call them "friend," and they cannot be my coach.

Note that friendships have a tendency to become toxic relationships when you are and have always been better than the other person at everything. In this context, friendship is more than just a casual acquaintanceship or someone you see every so often—a friend is someone you interact with at least somewhat regularly. If you are spending extensive time with someone who has absolutely no way in which they are/have been superior to you (e.g., socially, relationships, kindness, financially, mentally, specific subject matters, physically, etc.), then one or both of you may develop resentment towards the other one. They might start thinking that you are a know-it-all or you have a superiority complex, and you might start feeling like they are a leech and/or a time sink. In either of these scenarios, the relationship will become toxic. It has been my experience that these types of toxic relationships will make it more difficult for you to achieve your dreams. So be careful who you call "friend."

This logic also applies to who you choose to date and marry. Any person you spend significant time with should have something that they can deposit in you AND you should have something that you are depositing in them. Ultimately, whomever you are in a relationship with will become your ultimate coach. They become that

> "Next to who you choose as Lord & Savior, who you choose to marry is the single greatest determinate of your long-term success."
> Dr. Tanya Dugat-Wickliff

most important core member of your team of two, so do not take that decision lightly. Whomever you choose to be your closest coach and confidant can make or break you, so choose wisely.

- MENTORS -

Now that we have covered your coaches, next let's talk about your mentors. A mentor is a person who is or has been where you are going. As such, this person can and will help you navigate the pitfalls you will encounter in your professional life. All coaches with relevant work experience can act as mentors, but MOST MENTORS

SHOULD NOT BE TREATED LIKE COACHES.

Coaches can hear the good, the bad, and the ugly of your thoughts and opinions. In contrast, it is a huge mistake to approach your mentor with things that can be categorized as petty or overly personal. Your mentor does not need to know how much you hate your supervisor or hear your extensive ranting about your annoying in-laws.

I am not saying that you cannot have personal conversations with your mentor—having general conversations about your family or a shared interest is completely acceptable. Additionally, it is important to find someone you can have candid conversations with about difficult professional questions, like:

How to best navigate starting a family with your work responsibilities, how to broach the subject of working remotely to better handle family health issues, when it is an appropriate time to report the inappropriate behavior of a supervisor to their supervisor, etc.

"Associate with men of good quality if you esteem your own reputation; for it is better to be alone than in bad company."
Pres. George Washington

However, you never want to engage in angry ranting, nor do you want to perpetually complain (especially about personal matters) to your mentors. This is disrespectful of their time, and you risk being perceived as a nuisance to be ignored rather than a protégé to be guided.

Additionally, do not go to your mentor for advice you really don't want. I myself have been guilty of going to friends for "advice" when I really just want them to affirm the course of action that I already plan to take. This practice can be acceptable with friends, acquaintances, and even coaches, but it is not acceptable to do this with your mentor or your sponsor. If your mentor strongly recommends that you do or don't do something and you ignore that recommendation, then you may make a lasting negative impression on them. This kind of impression is something you may never be able to recover from. That does not mean you have to treat everything your mentor says as the gospel truth or that you can't go against their recommendations for valid reasons, but if it becomes clear to your mentor that you made a decision before asking for their advice and no logic is going to sway you, then they will feel like you are wasting their time.

- SPONSORS -

Your sponsor is the person with access that can open doors for you. When I say "access," what do I mean? The first thing you may think of is money and other tangible resources. While wealth does give you "access," I define the term more broadly: access is the ability to be heard and listened to by people with relevant decision-making authority. Thus, even though things like money can help someone *get* access, your sponsor does not actually need money to *have* access. Additionally, all people with money don't necessarily have the influence to impact decision-making.

To illustrate this explanation, consider the president/CEO of a Fortune 500 company and the sitting President of the United States. If you could only pick one of them to help you get your dream job, who would it be? Even though most company presidents and CEOs make significantly more money than the majority of the United States' past Presidents have made, the President of the United States has far more access—one phone call from the President of the United States could get you an audience with almost any major decision-maker in the world.

For your sponsor, you want someone who has both access and a willingness to use their access to help you achieve your goals and dreams. Your sponsor is a person who can get you major opportunities that you would not otherwise be considered for. You want a sponsor who is actually willing to make those kinds of calls on your behalf.

A sponsor is typically the most difficult to find because so few people have that kind of influence. You can have multiple coaches and mentors, and you will continuously find more of them as you advance through life. Yet, most people only get a couple of opportunities to have a true sponsor. Therefore, if you find a sponsor who is willing to take you under their wing, foster that relationship.

There is no perfect recipe for attaining a sponsor. While getting coaches and mentors is typically accomplished by a straightforward conversation or participation in a particular program, sponsors are different. Typically, your sponsors are not people you choose, they are people who choose you. Thus, typically you attain the opportunity to acquire sponsors by being high-performing and visible in your company and community. When people of influence see your strong work ethic, ambition, and good attitude, they seek you out.

Notice that I said you "attain the opportunity to acquire a sponsor." You can earn a first meeting with a potential sponsor and may even earn the right to have them as a mentor. However, sponsoring an up-and-coming talent is not a requirement, nor is there anything you can do to truly demand or deserve sponsorship. This relationship forms when a person of influence takes an interest in your long-term success. Although you can't control when or if this particular relationship forms, it is your responsibility to foster these types of relationships.

Fostering a relationship with a sponsor is a very different experience. For one thing, these are people who have very limited time, so you should have very concise updates when you meet with them. On most occasions, before any planned meeting with my sponsor (whether formal or informal), I meet with at least one of my coaches and one of my mentors to refine what I want to talk about. You might only see your sponsor once or twice a year, so it is important to make a good impression and use your time productively.

More importantly, do not treat your sponsor like a mentor (and especially don't treat them like a coach!). They are not the people who are supposed to help you with daily or even monthly problems. When growing a sponsorship relationship, you want to pay particularly close attention to the section of this chapter on Relationship Management. If you are going to ask your sponsor for help, it should be for a major issue or significant ask.

For example, if you are trying to figure out how to deal with your annoying boss, that is a question for your mentor. If you are having difficulty securing an interview for a prestigious position at a new company, that is a potential conversation for your sponsor.

- CHEERLEADERS -

There is one more person I think every team should have, and that is your personal cheerleader. As the title implies, they are in your life to spur you to success. This person may not be good for advice and may have no idea what it takes for you to accomplish your goals. However, regardless of what you do in life, they are there with a kind and uplifting word. These are the people who most relish in your success and consistently cheer you through your setbacks.

Do not mistake a fan for a cheerleader. When you start accomplishing more of your goals and working your way towards your dream, you are going to catch some people's attention. You may have some people noticing your success and congratulating you. But these are not your cheerleaders, these are your fans. Cheerleaders do not just pat you on the back when you are doing well—they also continue to be a positive encouraging force when things are going badly. Fans cheer for what has already happened and base their cheering on anticipated outcomes; cheerleaders cheer without regard to how well or badly you are doing. That is what differentiates a fan from a cheerleader, and you want the latter on your team, not the former.

Why is this distinction important? Have you ever sat through a game that was a clear blowout from the beginning? I had the great misfortune of going to one of the smallest Division 1 universities in the country and the smallest Division 1 football school in Texas (Rice University). What that means is that our small school, with fewer than 80,000 alumni living and dead, plays against some of the best nationally ranked football teams in the nation. Some of these teams represent universities with more than 50,000 students on campus each year. Our football defeats are so well documented that when President John F. Kennedy announced the national effort to put a man on the moon, he equated this seemingly impossible task to Rice University playing the University of Texas in football on a yearly basis. As such, I have watched my team take some astronomical defeats on the gridiron.

What normally happens when a team starts losing badly? The fans stop cheering and start leaving. Have you ever seen a cheerleader leave the field while the game was still in progress? No matter how horrible the blowout is, the cheerleaders keep cheering in a seemingly forlorn hope that their team will recover. And every so often, they do!

Similarly, when things are going badly for you, you need cheerleaders in your corner who will not abandon you when you are down. These are the people who will hope against hope and still lift your spirits in the face of almost certain defeat. This is important, because no matter how self-motivated and independent you are, it is hard to keep fighting what feels like a losing battle. Much like the effective reward system discussed earlier in this book, a cheerleader can keep you motivated to work even when the outcome seems bleak. In doing so, a good cheerleader can help you snatch success from the jaws of defeat.

Another important function of a cheerleader is to help you refocus after a setback. No matter how good you are at what you do, you are going to make mistakes. Whether it is in your professional life, personal life, or academic life, there will be times when you do something you consider to be "bone-headed" or "idiotic." The problem with those types of mistakes is that we have a tendency to fixate on them. In doing so, we can slip into a rut and start making more mistakes. Your cheerleader is the one who is going to get you to refocus after those bone-headed mistakes.

For me, my greatest cheerleader is my oldest brother Jamar. I can go to my Mom for mentoring and my brother Ray for coaching, but in those situations where I just need to be cheered up, Jamar is my go-to guy. Whether it was a bad breakup, a crappy boss, a major mistake on an assignment, or a bad grade, he has always been the eternal optimist who consistently cheers me up and cheers me on. No matter what endeavor I undertake, he is the person I most count on to give me the unyielding moral support that I need to get back to working towards my goals.

- RELATIONSHIP MANAGEMENT -

Navigating the process of growing your team can be difficult. I have made numerous mistakes when trying to foster relationships with potential team members. I told you earlier about losing a potential sponsor at a law firm because I did not do enough to grow that relationship. I have also lost mentors and coaches because of shortcomings in my relationship management. It is a learning process, so don't get discouraged if you have a few setbacks. Just always learn from your mistakes and do better if ever you are presented with a similar circumstance.

Even though mastering how to communicate with your team and manage your relationships is something you will have to figure out through trial and error, I do want to take this time to share three things that have helped me in my interpersonal networking and team building: 1. *Develop your personal communication style*, 2. *Properly implement code-switching*, and 3. *Don't get inappropriately casual with your communications.*

> "We cannot change the cards we are dealt, just how we play the hand."
> Prof. Randy Pausch

Relationship management is a difficult thing to master because it is a skill set that each person has to customize for themselves. A mistake people often make is to believe that the way someone else communicates with a particular person is the way *they* should communicate with them, too. However, everything does not work the same for everyone. The relationship-building tactics that work best for you are going to be determined by how people perceive you. That perception is influenced by both your and their gender, age, appearance, culture, religion, knowledge, experiences (both mutually and individually), and a host of other factors. Even something as basic as your height can drastically change the way you should interact with people. A short person can say something that is seen as cute, whereas if a gigantic person says the exact same thing and in the same way, it is seen as intimidating.

A real-world example of this is my mom and I. Mom has been one of my greatest mentors and coaches. She has taught me numerous things about relationship-building and networking. I have learned numerous networking tactics and principles that work universally (e.g., be respectful of people's time, be an active listener, don't be dismissive, etc.), but some of the relationship-building tactics that work best for me as a young male are very different than the tactics that work best for Mom. When I am direct and blunt, it is seen as admirable; if she were to be equally as direct and blunt, it would be seen as anger. Conversely, because people see her as a maternal figure, even in the world of work, she is able to use an "office mom" persona to influence and endear herself to people around her. Whereas, because of our gender and age differences, if I attempted to adopt that same persona, I would be seen as creepy.

Make sure that you are being honest with yourself and doing an honest evaluation of how you are likely to be perceived; then conduct yourself accordingly. And if you do not know how your actions or words might be perceived, utilize your coaches for honest feedback.

One perception I struggle with is that because of my academic background and credentials, people have a strong tendency to assume I am trying to be condescending. Even in college, I could say the exact same thing as some of my friends, but it would be perceived differently. Keep in mind that this perception has little to nothing to do with actually having met me. As with a lot of negative perceptions, they are often formed based on previous negative encounters with other people. Thus, you may have no control over someone else's perceptions. These types of preexisting biases are prevalent and oftentimes random. However, you are the one responsible for your success, so you must adapt and thrive

> "I don't really care so much what people say about me because it usually is a reflection of who they are."
> Prince Rogers Nelson

despite whatever preconceived biases people might have about you.

For me, when I developed my personal communication style, I made sure to go out of my way to be relatable. This counteracts the tendency of people to assume I am stuck-up or condescending based on my background. Also, because people assume that most accomplished people have a bad attitude, I gain the benefit of being seen as a rare combination of being a high achiever and having a positive attitude. Thus, I use their preexisting biases as a way to improve my overall reputation.

> "We are not what other people say we are. We are who we know ourselves to be..."
> Laverne Cox

Unfortunately, we have likely all been harshly reminded of the negative stereotypes and perceptions people have of us. Whether it is prejudgments based on your appearance, the way you speak, an immutable expression of your DNA, your nationality, your religion, having the "misfortune" of being born on the wrong side of the track, or any number of other things that have nothing to do with your character, we have all experienced people's biases. It is not your job to change everyone's biases and perception—your responsibility is simply to succeed. Although it is not always an easy task, I encourage you to find ways to use these biases to your advantage. Remember, regardless of what people think of you—good or bad—you must learn to use those perceptions to get your desired outcomes (i.e., success and the support of great coaches, mentors, and sponsors).

Not only should you customize your overall communication style to address how people generally perceive you, you also need to specifically customize your interactions with individuals. The way you interact with people may change significantly based on who they are. This is sometimes called "code-switching." Code-switching is a communication mechanism that's often employed by people who are bilingual, bicultural, and/or of cultural minorities, where the speaker will change their lexicon and communication style to what is most relatable and understandable for their audience. Put simply, code-switching is speaking the language, dialect, or lexicon of whomever you are talking to. It often takes years of practice and refinement to master this communication technique; however, once mastered, it is a powerful tool in your relationship-building arsenal.

However, in order to be able to effectively code-switch, you must actually seek to understand the people you are communicating with. If you are unwilling to understand the way a particular person or group communicates and are not willing to understand their cultural or social norms, you cannot expect that they will want to work with you. Oftentimes, such ignorance of others can lead to unintentionally insulting behavior. And any time you make someone feel disrespected or unimportant, that is someone who will not want to help you in the future.

An example of code-switching that we have all probably engaged in is when communicating with people of different generations. The way you communicate with your friends is (or at least should be) different than the way you communicate with your grandparents and their peers. There are certain phrases and words you will not use and certain communication styles you will adopt (e.g., talking more slowly, using less abrasive tones, communicating with more subdued interactions, etc.). This is a basic form of code-switching that we can all generally relate to. Mastering this technique when communicating across cultural, generational, racial, and gender boundaries will have a profoundly positive impact on your ability to assemble a diverse and supportive team.

The last—and, in some ways, the most important— technique I believe everyone should have in their team-building tool set is to avoid getting too casual. As someone who has worked in both academia and the private sector, this is a mistake I have seen so many young professionals and students make! I cannot count the times I have seen the look of disgust come across a colleague's face when being introduced to someone 20 to 30 years their junior and the young person says something like "Hey, Bob."

With most people, especially people with doctorates and/or fancy titles they have worked years to acquire, being addressed so informally by a stranger will permanently sour their opinion of that person. Whereas, for the people who prefer to be addressed informally, there is no negativity associated with someone saying, "Hello, Dr. Johnson." In this context, they would have an immediate positive perception of you being a respectful individual, and they would likely reply, "Nice to meet you, but please just call me Bob."

Another form of informality that I often see is treating work environments like casual social gatherings. Whenever you are interacting with a mentor/sponsor or a potential mentor/sponsor, you should treat those encounters as if you are on the job. This is not the time to "let your hair down," overindulge in alcohol, or air any personal issues. Have fun and be social, but maintain your composure. You never want to be the person in your office whom everyone is talking about the next week.

Note that maintaining formality is not the same thing as being stiff. You can still have fun; just make sure you are not doing anything that reflects poorly on your character or professionalism. Additionally, sharing personal details about yourself can be a way to endear you to a potential mentor/sponsor, but you never want to share anecdotes that are inappropriate or sketchy. Remember, you never know when potential sponsors are vetting you.

If you master these three aspects of communication (i.e., customize your style, code-switch when needed, and don't be too informal), you will be well on your way to building an impressive roster of coaches, mentors, and sponsors.

Ultimately, the objective of your interactions, especially with mentors and sponsors, is to maintain and grow your relationship capital. Relationship capital is an intangible asset—it is a reflection of how much goodwill you have built up in a particular relationship. The amount of goodwill or relationship capital that you maintain is important, because it determines how much someone is going to be willing to do on your behalf. The more relationship capital you have in a relationship, the more someone is willing to do for you. However, any time someone does something for you or you do something that irks/offends them, you spend some of your relationship capital.

How do you build relationship capital? There are numerous ways to build your relationship capital with someone: helping them when they are in need, delivering on your promises, showing respect, being reliable, showing concern, and generally doing/saying anything that endears you to someone or that improves your reputation in their eyes. This could be as big as saving someone in a tough situation or as small as remembering someone's birthday. Even being from the same alma mater or part of the same fraternity/sorority can be a way to develop rapport and increase your relationship capital with someone.

It is, however, important to realize that your relationship capital is a limited resource that can run out. If you are constantly asking for something and never reciprocating in any way, your relationship will become "bankrupt." In that case, you will become one of those toxic relationships I spoke of previously, and you will likely lose your relationship with that person. Once destroyed, a relationship is extremely hard to redevelop. So make sure that you utilize your team efficiently, and above all else, don't waste people's time! Wasting someone's time is often the quickest way to bankrupt your relationship with them.

Other ways in which people bankrupt their relationships are to endanger someone else's life, livelihood, or their ability to provide for their family. Put simply, if your actions start to negatively impact someone's cash flow, then they will likely sever their relationship with you. In an age of social media, one of the quickest ways you can endanger someone else's livelihood is to become a controversial figure via problematic posting. Brands and people who associate with unsavory individuals often see a significant reduction in their earnings.

Keep in mind, if you are aiming for a lofty and/or lucrative goal, your social media presence is more about business than fun. People have lost millions of dollars because of stupid tweets and questionable pictures. Don't be one of those people! Assume that anything you share or send on the internet (even in private chats or text messages) is going to end up being public. Don't derail your life for a few likes, retweets, or comments.

In addition to wasting someone's time or endangering their revenue, requiring forgiveness is a quick way to run out of relationship capital. When you insult or harm someone, them forgiving you is a major expenditure of your relationship capital with them. Be mindful of how your words and actions impact those around you. If someone is put in a position where they must forgive your actions or apologize on your behalf, you are likely to lose credibility (e.g., relationship capital) with that person. Additionally, repeatedly needing forgiveness (especially for the same offense) is a sure way to bankrupt your relationships.

Although forgiveness consumes relationship capital, something far worse is not admitting when you are wrong. My personal advice is this: when you know you have done wrong to someone, sincerely apologize, and do so quickly. Failing to apologize for an extended period of time and/or lying about what you have done is only going to consume more of your relationship capital when you are caught. This advice applies to both personal and professional relationships. For example, it is a known and documented fact that when someone feels wronged and receives a sincere apology, they are less likely to pursue legal action and more likely to settle for a smaller sum of money.

Similar to apologizing, you can better grow and preserve your relationship capital when you quickly identify pointless battles and graciously concede defeat. In general, it harms your overall success and depletes your relationship capital if you are pigheaded in your pursuit of meaningless victories. Not only does it show undesirable personality traits, but it also demonstrates to your team that you are poor at managing resources and relationships, which makes them less likely to trust you. I have seen people ruin their careers and lives because they are not willing to concede a simple defeat on their pathway to overall success. Whether it is something as simple as letting your egocentric boss win at a meaningless game or something as complex as conceding an easy negotiation point so that you have more negotiation power

> "People will forget what you said, people will forget what you do, but people will never forget how you made them feel."
> Maya Angelou

in tougher confrontations, a well-selected "defeat" can pave the path to overall victory.

Throughout history, we have seen examples of leaders who depleted their relationship/political capital by pursuing foolhardy victories and who then ultimately wound up losing the overall conflict (e.g., General Santa Anna and the Alamo, the U.S. government and the war in Vietnam, Russia and the Cold War's arms race, etc.). Or thinking personally, I am sure you have seen people turn potential friends into enemies because they doled out unnecessarily embarrassing defeats. If I may use an old adage, "Don't win the battle to lose the war." It is an invaluable skill to learn when to take a short-term loss in order to preserve your relationship capital with your preexisting team and gain more relationship capital with potential team members.

It is important to properly manage your relationship capital with your coaches, mentors, and sponsors. In general, these relationships have a major impact on your ability to succeed at your goals. So you want to ensure that you have high-quality coaches, mentors, and sponsors who think highly of you.

As previously stated, deciding who will be on your team can have a profound impact on your life. These are the people who will guide you through your personal, spiritual, academic, and professional journeys. They will correct you when you are wrong, support you when you are weak, and be there for you when you are in need. Thus, the people on your team will influence your success and

> "You can't hang out with chickens and expect to soar with eagles."
> Joel Osteen

the person you become. Some of these influences may start off subtle, but will eventually get more substantial.

Back home, they would say "Hot and cold can't mix." The metaphor is that if ever you put hot and cold water into the same container, they meet in the middle and become the same temperature. Thus hot water and cold water can't interact continuously with each other while remaining the same. What they are saying with this metaphor is that whomever you interact with the most will cause you to become more like them and vice versa. Whether it is a subtle change or an extreme one, whoever is on your team is going to change you.

Also, because association breeds assimilation, who you surround yourself with will tell people a lot about you. People assume that "birds of a feather flock together." Thus, the people around you will assume that you share the characteristics of the people you flock towards. If you associate with people who are not doing anything with their lives or are considered untrustworthy, people will assume that you are the same. Conversely, if your team is filled with good, ambitious, and dedicated members, then people will assume you are of good character and are ambitious and dedicated. Thus, over time, the team you surround yourself with can drastically alter your life trajectory for better or for worse.

Choose your team wisely!

Chapter 13:
Learn From Mistakes: Yours & Others

Mistakes are not the enemy of success, repeating them is! Anyone who has done anything worthwhile has encountered setbacks, made mistakes, and/or regretted past decisions. Making mistakes does not stop you from being successful. In fact, as long as you learn from your mistakes and don't dwell on them, mistakes can be an invaluable part of success.

Former Texas Governor Ann Richards said it best: "…we all have to learn from our mistakes, and we learn from those mistakes a lot more than we learn from the things we succeeded in doing."

When you succeed, you have only used your previous knowledge to identify a way to achieve success. Additionally, you are less likely to critically assess your performance or actions in circumstances that result in your success. Therefore, the only thing you glean from successful situations is that your approach worked in that circumstance. However, next time, if any one condition, situation, or occurrence changes, you don't know if your approach will be successful.

> *"If you are really good, your greatest failure is the beginning of the greatest thing in your life."*
> Maverick Carter

Making a mistake is different. First and foremost, you are far more likely to analyze your overall performance when you make a mistake. When you miss a shot, answer a question wrong, forget a key detail, or somehow come up short in crucial moments, you replay those moments over and over again. Because of this fact, we are far less likely to remember our successes than our failures.

For example, I took an algebra test in the eighth grade. I cannot tell you anything about the test now other than when solving for the x-intercept of a parabola, there are two solutions. Why after more than 15 years do I remember that statement? Because I lost a ridiculous amount of points on that exam for forgetting to put "+/-" in front of my answers (i.e., "x= +4 AND -4"). Keep in mind that I still got over 80% of that exam correct, but I honestly could not tell you anything else that was on that test. This is because mistakes are more deeply etched into our memories than most successes are.

If you are wise, you will use this phenomenon to your advantage. Don't just remember the mistakes, but remember how to avoid them in the future! A wise person will do everything in their power to make sure they never make the same mistake again.

> "Success is a lousy teacher. It seduces smart people into thinking they can't lose."
>
> Bill Gates

In my subsequent 12 years of taking math classes and solving complex equations, one thing I never forgot was that there are always two solutions to parabolic equations. I made numerous mistakes in the course of my math career, but I never forgot to write down that second solution. This phenomenon is the reason I say, "People don't succeed in spite of failures, they succeed because of them."

The only time a failure truly derails you is when you allow it to make you quit. Losing can be a lonely and painful feeling. That moment when you put forth your best effort, but it just wasn't good enough can hurt. And I assure you that at some point, you are going to come up short in your pursuits. Whether it is personally, academically, or professionally, we all "take an L" every once in a while. However, those shortcomings do not define you; rather, how you respond will determine your legacy.

However, losses, failures, and setbacks hurt have a strong tendency to make you want to curl up into a ball and never try anything again. How do you get past that feeling so you can learn from your mistakes and resume the pursuit of your dream?

The exact process will be different for each person. That said, I believe it can be broken down into three steps: 1. *Grieve on a timetable*, 2. *Reward yourself for the effort*, and 3. *Resume working as soon as possible*.

A major loss or mistake can be tough to cope with. Whenever we lose something important to us, we need time to grieve over the loss. Whether you need to cry, talk to someone, go to therapy, or write your feelings out, do whatever it takes to grieve your loss. The only limitations are that it must not be harmful to you, someone else, or your ability to achieve your dream; *it should be appropriate*; and *you should avoid things you will regret later.*

Additionally, all of your grieving should be in a finite time period. If we allow ourselves to grieve indefinitely, we end up in a rut. First you are grieving because of your initial loss, then your grieving makes you miss out on additional opportunities, and then you grieve for those lost opportunities. If you get stuck in that cycle, it can be never-ending. So set an appropriate time table that allows you to grieve but still makes sure you are ready to achieve your long-term goals.

The second step in the process is to utilize your reward system. Remember, your reward system is a reward for the effort, not the outcome. Thus, you must give yourself some form of reward to acknowledge your hard work. And even if you don't have an established reward, do something fun to take your mind off of things. The goal of this stage is just to find a reason to smile and have a hearty laugh. Laughter is therapeutic! The first time you are able to laugh after a heart-wrenching experience is the first time you will feel like yourself.

For example, my dad's death was a huge personal setback. Although it was not a mistake I made, it was still a loss I had to get through. After his passing, I was semi-forced to play some games with family and friends. The first genuine laugh I had was the first time I felt like I could be me again. Whether you are getting past something like the loss of a family member or a failure connected to a major milestone, finding your joy is how you find yourself.

Once you have grieved and laughed, it is time to work. Out in the country, we are taught that if you fall off a horse, you have to get right back up there. I know you may have heard this phrase used figuratively, but in Texas, it is a very literal phrase: if you fall off of a horse and allow too much time to pass, you are likely to develop a fear. Eventually, the five-foot-high saddle starts to feel like it's 50 feet high, and the gentle horse begins to look like a monster. Whereas, if you immediately get back on the horse, you stop trauma before it forms.

Similarly, after a major loss or setback, it can be easy to become traumatized by the experience. Something that used to be so natural can become frightening, and a wall of fear can slowly but surely build. You start thinking that your dreams are impossible and the obstacles insurmountable. The best way to combat those thoughts is to "get back on the horse" and start working again. Regardless of whether you are an athlete going back to the gym, a writer picking up a pen, a speaker getting back in front of an audience, or a student picking back up a textbook, you must try to get back to your previous routine as quickly as possible.

However, do not fault yourself if the first few times are rough. Think of mental injuries like physical injuries. When you suffer a major physical injury, you have to go through rehab to get back full function. Rehab is doing the motions you would normally do, but at a lower rate/level. This is you rehabbing your ability to pursue your dreams. You need to get back into your routine as soon as possible, even if it is uncomfortable and difficult. Just as with rehab, you might not even be able to do everything you usually can, but working though it is a part of the process of recovering from a setback.

> "I don't like to lose at anything... Yet I've grown most not from victories, but setbacks. If winning is God's reward, then losing is how he teaches us."
> Serena Williams

206

Once you make it past your setback, you will then be in a perfect vantage point to review and learn from your previous mistakes. Then use what you learned to persistently pursue your ambitions.

———————

For most of us, learning from our own mistakes is self-evident and not a particularly revolutionary idea. However, when you are trying to achieve an ambitious dream, learning from your own mistakes cannot be the only way you learn. There are some mistakes you cannot afford to make because they are both figuratively and literally fatal. As such, there are some lessons you need to learn through the experiences of others.

"A hard head makes a soft behind." This quote has been a warning to children throughout the South for generations. If you had the great misfortune of hearing this uttered from your mother, grandmothers, aunts, or any adult, it meant you were very close to getting a spanking. What does this have to do with you achieving success?

The reason the statement begins with "A hard head" is because it was only used when you were given instructions that you ignored. When you ignored the warnings of your elders, you were inviting calamity in the form of a belt across your backside. In other words, failing to heed the instructions or warnings of those who came before you can oftentimes result in unnecessary harm. This is the same logic that gave rise to the statement "Those who do not learn from history are doomed to repeat it."

Every class you have ever taken, every training you have ever gone through, and every lesson someone has ever attempted to teach you inside or outside of the classroom was an attempt to tell you how to avoid a mistake that someone else has previously made. I had the great honor of being invited to speak to the men and women of the 1st Special Operations Wing of the U.S. Air Force. There, they do not have the option of each person learning only from their own mistakes, because with every operation they undertake, the lives of so many people hang in the balance. So they drill and train on a daily basis. Similarly, you should be training yourself daily and absorbing lessons others had to learn through trial and error.

Remember, time is the only resource in life that you need for every accomplishment and that you cannot replenish once you lose it. If you want to maximize your success and achieve lofty dreams in your lifetime, you do not have the time to repeat mistakes. Put bluntly, if you want to accomplish any worthwhile dream, you cannot waste time. Though life is a great teacher, it is far more time-efficient to learn your lessons in a proactive manner. This means that not only should you learn from your own mistakes and try never to repeat the same ones, but you should also learn from the mistakes of others so that you do not repeat those, either.

How do you effectively learn from the mistakes of others?

Do your homework. There is a surprising amount of literature out there about navigating everything from raising a child to starting a business. More often than not, you'll find plenty of published material, instructional videos, and readily available information about the goal you are pursuing. Whether it is attending a seminar, watching an instructional video, or reading a book about a specific subject matter, you should be willing to consume all of the available information that pertains to what you are trying to accomplish.

Additionally, sometimes the simplest way to get inside information about the route you are taking is to ask the people who have already been there. Even when you are doing something that is considered novel, there will be aspects of your journey that resemble or are identical to the journeys of other people. I have never met another person who has a BS in engineering, a JD, and a PhD in engineering, and I have never heard of anyone getting all three degrees before turning 26 years old. Thus, there was no one person who could advise me on every potential pitfall of my journey. However, I know plenty of people with a BS in engineering. I have three lawyers in my extended family. And once my mom got her PhD

> "See or make a mistake once and it becomes a lesson; afterwards, make that same mistake and it becomes a choice."
> Dr. Cortlan J. Wickliff

in engineering, I had an in-house resource to help navigate the pitfalls of a PhD program. So at each stage of my journey, I found somebody who had already accomplished that segment of my journey.

This is one of the reasons why it is important to build a good team of coaches and mentors. Without the candid and honest advice of my team, I would have never accomplished as much as I have.

Find someone who has achieved or attempted to achieve a dream or goal you also want to achieve and then ask them about their journey:

"What are some things you wish you had known when you began your journey?" "If you had it to do again, what would you do differently?" "What would you do the same?" "What are your regrets?" "What was the most helpful and the most harmful to you achieving your goal?" "Do you have any recommendations for me?"

You may be surprised by who will take time out of their schedule to tell you about themselves. We are often afraid to approach people to ask them for advice because we assume that they will say "no." However, remember, if all you have to fear is them saying "no," go for it! The potential benefit that you could gain from their years of experience greatly outweighs the downside of potentially hearing the word "no."

It is worth noting that I have never been turned down for a conversation with anyone when I have asked them about their personal journey. In my experience, when someone is genuinely interested in them, people feel flattered and want to share. I might have had to be persistent if they were busy, but ultimately, the people I reached out to felt excited to provide guidance.

> "Don't become too narrow. Live fully. Meet all kinds of people. You'll learn something from everyone."
> Yuri Kochiyama

Remember to do an honest self-assessment of how people perceive you and then utilize those perceptions to your advantage. For all of my readers who are high school and college students, this is the best time for you to try to grow your team of coaches and mentors. Established professionals perceive you as malleable young minds and potential protégés and often will provide a lot of opportunities for you to be mentees. Take advantage of the ability to get funding for unpaid internships and research opportunities and also seek out paid internships, co-ops, and research opportunities. Those represent a unique competitive advantage in that they will allow you to have face time with successful people. And where there is not already an established mentorship/internship program, be bold enough to call and email people to informally shadow them.

For readers who are more career-seasoned and already have a network, your approach will probably be different. Getting the opportunity to gain advice from knowledgeable people is something that is worth spending some relationship capital on. Utilize your existing network and resources to get meetings with people.

Additionally, for all readers, know what you bring to the table. Just like you want advice from them about some aspect of your growth and development, they may want advice from you. However, that requires you to take a full inventory over all of who you are. For me, not all of the meetings I have are related to my academic and professional skill set. I have had several entrepreneurs meet with me to get my advice as a life-long Texan on how to break into the Texas market, for example. I have had older people want to get my advice on developing youth outreach initiatives. I have even had very lengthy conversations with potential mentors during which they wanted me to weigh in on how my faith was impacted by going to college. There are so many facets of you outside of your education and your career! Each of those facets represents a connection point to potentially engage with an advisor.

Notice that I suggested talking to both people who have achieved and *attempted to achieve* one of your goals or dreams. We oftentimes ignore people whom we do not perceive as being successful enough. In general, that is a huge mistake, but it is especially a mistake when you are trying to learn from others. In the South, we have a saying: "A broken clock is right two times a day." This is a colloquialism that tells us you can learn something from everyone—regardless of how seemingly "broken" they are, everyone has some nuggets of wisdom to share. Be open to receiving good advice from unexpected sources.

We have a strong tendency to believe that the only people who can help us are people who are perfect. However, just because someone makes a mistake doesn't mean that they have

> "Sometimes the road less traveled is less traveled for a reason."
> Jerry Seinfeld

nothing to offer you. The pathway to success is narrow and has numerous pitfalls. Just because someone tripped midway down the path doesn't mean they can't tell you how to start your journey or give you some tips for success.

Let's say you want to start a business and you know someone who ran an otherwise successful business that failed because of not keeping good tax records. This person can give you great advice about avoiding mistakes like failing to keep track of vendor expenses or filing improper withholdings. Additionally, even though their accounting was problematic, other aspects of their business model could have been done well. Were they good at marketing, product development, sales, recruiting, fundraising, multimedia development, etc.?

> "If it's flipping hamburgers at McDonald's, be the best hamburger flipper in the world. Whatever it is you do you have to master your craft."
> Calvin "Snoop Dogg" Broadus, Jr.

Look at a business venture like the Fyre Festival. Their accounting, project management, and planning were atrocious; however, the Fyre Festival marketing campaign and fundraising were exceptional. If you pair that type of viral social media marketing campaign with a quality product, solid planning, and better project management, you could have a great business model. Remember, even when people fail overall, that does not mean they failed at every aspect of their attempt.

Conversely, just because someone is overall successful does not mean they are successful at everything they do. This is just a cautionary note when it comes to accepting advice from people. There is something called the Halo Effect—the tendency for an impression of someone in one area to influence the perception of them in another area. In other words, somebody being really good in one aspect of their life can cause others (and themselves) to believe that they are good in other aspects of their life even if that perception is not grounded in any evidence. Be careful not to fall victim to the Halo Effect! Critically assess the successes, strengths, and limitations of the people who are giving you advice.

For example, Warren Buffett is a wise and strategic businessman with a lot of knowledge to offer someone who is starting or growing a business. With decades of experience and a proven track record, you would be wise to capitalize on any opportunity you had to get his advice. However, what if instead of growing a business, you were trying to grow a social media following? Should he still be your go-to person?

If you answered "yes," you have fallen victim to the Halo Effect. Although Buffett's social media philosophy is good for growing your business (i.e., don't post often to avoid offending people and costing yourself money), it is not conducive to growing a social media following. For advice on growing social media, it would be far better to go to someone like Kristen Houghton (aka Kris Jenner). Kris Jenner has leveraged social media to create a multibillion-dollar fortune for herself and her children. She has managed the careers of all of her daughters, and if the people following each of her daughters on social media were a country, all of those countries would be one of the top 20 largest in the world (most would be in the top 10). Everyone has an area they excel in, and everyone has something to teach you. Just make sure you are learning the right lessons.

In addition to people being able to teach you from what they have done right, you can also learn from what people have done wrong—there is just as much value in learning what *not* to do as there is in learning what *to* do. And even if people cannot always articulate what you should do, most people can tell you or show you what not to do.

For example, some of the best advice I got for succeeding in college came from people who flunked out. Those were the people who told me to keep partying to a minimum, don't skip class, and get my books before classes started (along with several more tips for success).

Remember that learning what paths *not* to go down can be very helpful in locating your best route to success. Not only can you learn this lesson from people who have been down those "wrong paths," you can learn from people who avoided those paths altogether. As Jerry Seinfeld has said, "Sometimes the road less traveled is less traveled for a reason." When getting advice from people, don't just ask them why they did something, ask them why they *didn't* do something. They may have seen something you are missing, or there may be a circumstance of which you are unaware. Understanding why people chose to avoid certain paths in life can inform your decisions.

Also, you don't have to meet someone to learn from them. While I strongly encourage you to assemble a team of coaches and mentors, remember that those are not the only people you can learn from. Even if we never meet, reading this book is an opportunity to learn from me, my triumphs, my setbacks, and my mistakes. I encourage you to find other people who have written publications or have had publications written about them—learn from their stories, their words, and their examples.

Remember, my academic journey began unexpectedly with a book report on a civil rights leader. You never know what type of inspiration and motivation you can find from someone until you take the time to learn about them. As previously stated, the people you learn from don't have to be exactly like you nor do your pursuits need to be identical. Although his academic journey was inspiring and our academic timelines were similar, I knew early on that I had no desire to pursue the seminary education Dr. King attained—yet, his academic journey was still my inspiration. Thumb through the pages of history and seek out people who have done extraordinary things and/or who have inspired people you know. And seek out modern-day inspirations whose words you can regularly read and hear—with the prevalence of podcasts, social media, and recording devices, there is no shortage of access to modern-day role models.

If you are having trouble finding someone to inspire you, look through the pages of this book. There are over 100 people quoted in this book—they represent different races, genders, sexual orientations, backgrounds, religions, and ideologies (some of which I vehemently disagree with). Yet, every one of them have an interesting story to tell and plenty of lessons to teach you—their individual stories can show you the resilience to rise from homelessness to wealth, the contagious nature of courage in the face of adversity, the power of forgiveness, the impact of being true to your passion, etc. I strongly encourage you to choose a few people in this book, research them, and learn something from their successes and their shortcomings.

Remember, there are more paths to failure than there are to success, so don't feel the need to haphazardly stumble through the plethora of paths laid out before you. Use the wise counsel and examples set by others to avoid mistakes and identify your optimal paths to success.

> "...we all have to learn from our mistakes, and we learn from those mistakes a lot more than we learn from the things we succeeded in doing."
> Governor Ann Richards

Chapter 14:
Don't Share Your Dream with Everyone

I grew up in church. I was sometimes there four or five times a week. This was especially true after my dad passed. The church provided my mom with a convenient source of free babysitting and positive male role models. Whether or not you are Christian, you cannot deny the fact that the Bible is an incredibly intriguing read that has something for everyone. I personally love its stories, especially the ones from the Old Testament.

The Bible is full of stories you can derive life lessons from. I learned to be fearless from the stories of Daniel (Daniel 6:1-21), Shadrach, Meshach, and Abednego (Daniel 3:1-30). From Joshua, I learned that asking for the moon and the stars isn't an unreasonable expectation from life (Joshua 10:12-13). The story of David taught me that no matter how godly you are (Acts 13:22), you can make mistakes (2 Samuel 11:1-27). The primary lesson from this chapter is also something you can learn from the Bible, and that lesson is this: "Don't share your dream with everyone."

This lesson comes from one of my favorite Biblical stories, the story of Joseph in Genesis (Chapter 37-45). Joseph is sometimes called "The Dreamer." Through his dreams and interpretations of dreams, he saved his family and an entire nation of people from starvation.

Joseph was the eleventh of twelve brothers, yet he was his father's favorite son. His brothers resented him for this favoritism. Since he didn't have very high situational awareness, he compounded their agitation towards him by sharing his dream with them: in his dream, he lorded over them and all eleven of his brothers bowed at his feet.

This was especially problematic because, under the rules of their society, the eldest brother was supposed to be the leader. In an effort to prevent his dream from coming to pass and because his big mouth made them mad, Joseph's brothers sold him into slavery and faked his death. Ultimately, after years of triumph and misfortune, Joseph used his gift for interpreting dreams and his acquired skills of managing estates to work his way from being a slave and prisoner to being the second most powerful man in Egypt, right next to Pharaoh himself.

Eventually, his dream did come to pass and his brothers bowed at his feet. Still, because he had openly shared his dream, the route he took to get to his destination involved several pitfalls, near-death experiences, and setbacks. Treat this story as a cautionary tale. Had Joseph not so liberally shared his dream, he may not have angered his brothers and gotten sold into slavery.

You might ask, "Wasn't being a slave a necessary part of his journey?" While struggle can definitely be a character-building experience, Joseph's journey through slavery and prison might not have been a necessary hardship. In the story, Joseph becomes the second most powerful man in Egypt by correctly interpreting a dream that haunted Pharaoh. His interpretation of the dream saved Egypt and some surrounding areas from desolation at the hands of a horrible famine. It is quite possible he could have gotten to interpret that dream and could have gotten to that same position even without the hardship of his slavery and imprisonment.

Why did I share this story? Well, in addition to me just liking it so much, I wanted you to glean two lessons from the story of Joseph: 1. *Your past tragedy does not dictate your future trajectory* and 2. *You should not share your dream with everyone.*

Your tragedy does not dictate your trajectory! Anyone who has heard me give a speech has probably heard me say this phrase. It is a point I reiterate every chance I get, because learning this lesson has been vital to my success. What does the phrase mean?

> "One chance is all you need."
> Jesse Owens

First and foremost, the phrase means that where you start does not determine where you will finish. In life, having a rocky start to your journey or a difficult past does not stop you from accomplishing great things. A lot of people think that in order to succeed in life, you must have a pristine upbringing without any heartache or hardship. But that is just not true! Some of the greatest success stories in the world start from humble or even tragic beginnings.

Additionally, the phrase is meant to convey this: *You are not the sum total of your circumstances; you are the sum total of your choices.* You are not defined by the circumstances you were born into, what people have done to you, or what has happened/will happen to you in life. Instead, you are defined by how you choose to respond to those events. Professor Randy Pausch said it best: "We cannot change the cards we are dealt, just how we play the hand."

Do you feel like you have been dealt a horrible hand in life? That may be true. Now what?

It is still your responsibility to make the best use of what you are given in life. In the story of Joseph, he rose from being a slave and an ex-convict to being the second most powerful man in a foreign country. There are contemporary stories of people defying the odds every day.

> "I was set free because my greatest fear had been realized, and I still had a daughter who I adored, and I had an old typewriter and a big idea. And so rock bottom became a solid foundation on which I rebuilt my life."
> J.K. Rowling

Do not fall into the trap of statistics. As in, "Statistics say that growing up in a low-income household makes you X times more likely to go to jail."

Or "Statistics show that people with your condition have less than an X % chance of surviving."

Or even "Statistics show that people from your town have an X in 1,000 chance of graduating with a college degree."

There are statistics saying that the average height of an NBA player is about 6'7". The likelihood of being drafted if you are less than 6" tall is slim to none. However, Muggsy Bogues was only 5'3" and was drafted 12th overall in the 1987 NBA draft. He went on to have a successful fourteen-year-long-career in the NBA.

We live in a world where a deaf-blind woman became a Harvard lawyer, best-selling author, and world-renowned speaker and a man with no legs ran in the Olympics. Tyler Perry went from homelessness to owning a film studio, employing hundreds if not thousands of people, and being one of the wealthiest men in America. When Neil Armstrong was born, nobody had ever flown more than 8 ½ miles off the surface of the planet. Fewer than 30 years later, he flew over 230,000 miles above the Earth's surface to the moon. Before accomplishing these feats, how many statistics and how many people do you think said that those achievements would be impossible?

Don't let yourself be limited by what others say is possible or likely. Things that were once impossible happen on a daily basis.

Recognizing that you are the arbiter of your own destiny is an important lesson. However, the primary lesson that the story of Joseph taught me (and which is also the title of the chapter) is this: *Don't share your dreams with everyone.* Do not be the person who has your trajectory delayed or derailed because you shared your dreams or goals with the wrong person. When you are someone who is self-assured and confident in who you are and who you will become, then it is easy for you to genuinely be happy about the successes of others. People like that have difficulty comprehending that there are those who will genuinely despise you and wish you ill for no other reason than you achieving what you have worked hard for, but the unfortunate truth is that some people will try to stomp out your dreams, because you daring to reach for your dreams makes them feel bad about themselves. So be careful who you share your goals and dreams with.

I myself have been guilty of innocently oversharing with the wrong people. When I tell them, "I want to be an attorney," they hear, "You are trying to make more money than I will." Or when I say, "I am working on buying a home," they hear, "You think you are better than me." In these contexts, these types of people are letting their insecurities and personal issues negatively impact how they interact with others. You cannot control how people's insecurities make them feel, but you can control who you communicate with.

As you get more experience interacting in personal and professional scenarios, you will be able to better identify "red flags." Red flags are (sometimes subtle) indications that someone is not concerned with your well-being or wishes you ill. You will develop the ability to identify signs of ill intent, like insincere congratulations, backhanded compliments, and overly negative reactions to otherwise positive news. However, those red flags will not alert you to everyone. Additionally, it can be especially difficult to spot red flags in long-time friends and family members, especially when those people used to sincerely support you. So how do you tell the difference between who you should and shouldn't tell your dreams to?

> "Just because they say congratulations doesn't mean they are happy for you."
> Clayton Thomas

Rather than relying on an ability to identify who wishes you well and who wishes you ill, I have adopted a blanket rule: if the person isn't someone who can help you progress towards a goal or a dream, they don't really need to know about them. This was a lesson I wish I had learned sooner, because I used to have a nasty habit of telling people too much information. Though not as extreme, I have definitely experienced the "Joseph effect" of telling the wrong person my future plans and turning someone who could have been a helpful ally into a saboteur.

Let me give you a contemporary example of how this can play out to your detriment. My first time working for a technology company was when I worked at a leading medical device company. Even though this was after my fourth year in college, this was the first summer I could get a job working for a major company. (Up until that point, I had been under the age of 18, and companies would not hire me because of child labor laws.) I was excited to be applying my engineering skill set in the "real world," and I took on as many projects as I could. Though my technical skill set was on par with the skills of people three to five years older than me, I was still just an 18-year-old, and I had a lot to learn when it came to interpersonal skills.

One day, my supervisor asked me, "Where do you see yourself in five to ten years?"

The question caught me off guard since it seemingly came out of the blue. I said the first thing that came to mind, something along the lines of, "I like being able to manage hands-on projects, and I like the position you are in because you are close enough to the ground to get to do some interesting stuff. So I think I would like to be in a position like yours."

I, being the naïve teenager that I was at the time, didn't realize how that response was interpreted. What my manager heard was, "I want your job, and even though it took you 20 years to get here, I think I will be able to do it in five years."

Needless to say, our working relationship became far less friendly. Since I didn't realize what I had done, it took me a while to realize that I was being sabotaged. Suddenly, he became more critical of everything I did. One week, I was communicating too little; the next week, I was communicating too much. I would do something extremely well for an intern, but he would evaluate me against the full-time employees he had been working with for a decade or more. He skipped meetings with me and "forgot" to send me information for my projects. Any way that he could delay or sabotage me, he did.

Seemingly overnight, that went from the best job I had ever had to the most difficult. I had to dedicate a significant amount of time to finding ways to work around him. Because I shared a goal I should have kept to myself, my manager went from being a very helpful ally to being a continual roadblock.

In addition to the lesson of not sharing your goals with everyone, I want you to glean three things from this story. The first is that there are some things that take time and life experience to learn. The fact that you have not perfected yourself is not something that should weigh on you or in any way discourage you. We are all works in progress and should be learning daily. Yes, I was technically savvy well beyond my years and I could digest engineering and mathematics at an exceptional rate. Nevertheless, I was still a naïve teenager who had more to learn about the world. Remember, know what you are good at and improve what you aren't, but never fault yourself for where you are in your journey.

One of the things I also learned from this experience was that "I am not sure" and "I don't know" are acceptable answers. I have noticed that, especially when you are young, there is an artificial pressure to always have an answer for all questions—when we don't know the answer, we are taught to come up with something. Although

> "I can't gain anything off of anyone else not succeeding."
> Chance Bennett

this is good in schools and great on tests, it can be detrimental in the real world. At the time my supervisor asked me where I saw myself in five to ten years, my honest answer would have been "I am not sure." It is now ten years later, and I am in a position I could have never imagined, doing things I never expected. Had I been comfortable enough to speak honestly about my uncertainty instead of saying what I thought he wanted to hear, I would have been much better off.

This second lesson with a caveat. Not knowing exactly where you want to end up and/or how you want to get there does not absolve you of the responsibility to make progress towards a goal. As discussed in the "Start Building!" chapter, you can still set goals and work towards them even when you haven't decided on a dream. And you should be working to figure out what you want to do, either through trial and error, research, or honest self-assessment.

> "Work hard and never make excuses."
> Percy "Master P" Miller

The last lesson I want to impart from this story is that even when you mess up, your success is still your responsibility. In retrospect, I can see that I should have answered his question differently. That mistake made my job far more difficult. However, his attempts to sabotage me were not an acceptable excuse for me to fail to achieve my goals for that employment opportunity. I had to keep my objectives in mind, which were to complete all of my projects, exceed expectations, and leave a positive impression of myself. Despite the continuous hindrances, I recognized that my success is *my* priority and *my* responsibility. So even though it meant doing some extra work and spending extra time meeting with and updating his supervisors on my progress, I did what was necessary to make sure I achieved my goals.

Nevertheless, my journey would have been easier if I hadn't shared my dreams and goals with potential saboteurs. Put more simply, don't go out of your way to give haters additional reasons to hate. Although it is not always easy to identify somebody who is going to be one of your haters, there are a couple of principles that can help. Let's take a look at how you can identify people who can help you achieve your goals versus people you shouldn't tell your dreams to.

Going back to our previous section, identify your sponsors, coaches, mentors, and cheerleaders. If a person doesn't fall into one of those categories or have the potential to fall into one of those categories, they don't need to know what you are planning until it is done. In other words, the only people who need to know your goals and dreams are the people who you know have the ability and willingness to help you achieve them.

Now, just because somebody falls into one of the four categories, that doesn't mean they need to know everything you are planning. Be careful whenever you are directly or inadvertently telling somebody you are expecting to do something faster or better than them. Think about my experience with my manager. If the person is secure in themselves, they won't mind, but as previously discussed, a lot of people can take that as a challenge. I learned this from the mistake I made in telling my manager that I was going to get the same job he currently had in far less time. When it came time to talk to my PhD advisors, I knew I wanted to get a PhD in three years, but I did not tell any of my advisors that until after I had been approved for graduation.

Don't give people additional reasons to "hate on you" or be unnecessarily competitive with you. This is an especially good principle in circumstances where the person already looks down on you. Although it is unfortunate, we all have a pretty good idea of the people who think of themselves as being above others. Whether it be because of biases, racism, misogyny, nationalism, or just an overinflated ego, you will encounter people who believe that they are set apart from and above you. If possible, you really should avoid having these types of people in your inner circle to begin with; however, sometimes it is unavoidable that they will be. When you have a person like that as a member of your team, keep information exchange with them on an absolute-need-to-know-basis. This means that unless it is absolutely necessary for your progress or success to impart information to them, they do not need to know what you are planning or doing until after it is done.

When you are pursuing aggressive goals, you will occasionally rub some people the wrong way. You may hear things like:

> *"Who do you think you are?"*
> *"You're not better than me!"*
> *"That's impossible!"*
> *"You're dreaming!" etc.*

And maybe some people might even go out of their way to derail your progress. This sabotage and discouragement may even come from people you trust or love. Do not let this discourage you!

The important thing to remember is that regardless of what others do or say, you are responsible for your own success. And if you are like me and Joseph and accidentally let your mouth earn you some extra stumbling blocks, do not be discouraged! Go over them, around them, under them, or through them, but get to your dream!

> "I was once considered just a dreamer, but I paid my dues and turned so many doubters to believers."
> Justin "Big K.R.I.T." Scott

Chapter 15:
Every Ending is a New Beginning

If you are aggressive, thoughtful, and consistent in striving towards a goal, chances are, you will eventually achieve it! The chapters up until now have given you the tools you need to dream big and set & pursue goals effectively. I am confident that if you use the planning techniques, exercises, and methods outlined in this book, you will accomplish great things. Once you accomplish those goals and make your dream a reality, what's next?

My encouragement is for you to find new and challenging pursuits. I am a firm believer that having something to strive for and work towards is essential for a long, joyous life. I wish I could take credit for that nugget of wisdom, but it actually came from my Great Aunt Dimple Naomi Mims-Davis. She lived to be 94 years old, and could figuratively—and in some cases, literally—run circles around people 30 and 40 years her junior. Even in her 90s, she was known for throwing on her shades and cruising around Oklahoma City with the top dropped on her convertible.

As you can imagine, many people wanted to know the secret of how she remained so energetic. Her answer was simple: she stayed busy, although I don't think the word "busy" quite explains her mantra. I remember visiting her on one particular occasion. Keep in mind that she was between 88 and 90 years old at this point, and I was only 16 or 17. In my mind, I was going to do so many helpful things around her house, but the reality was that I barely got to wash a dish the entire time I was with her.

Any time she was awake, she was moving (cooking, cleaning, organizing, preparing for a church event, etc.). She was a cosmetologist by trade, and at 90 years old, she still did manicures and pedicures for a few customers she kept after retiring. Additionally, I could take up half of a chapter listing the ministries she either led or in which she was an active participant. And I am convinced I could publish an entire book about the people whose lives she impacted.

With the exception of the few catnaps she would take and the times she would indulge in watching the latest Tyler Perry play on her TV, there were not many times in a 24-hour period when she wasn't trying to do something. In general, whenever she finished a phase of her life, she readily picked up a new mission.

That does not mean work 24/7 until your dying day. Although she was busy, she was having fun! I know that working with church ministries and attending national church conventions might not be your definition of a good time, but she got joy out of it. Her philosophy was "Do all the good you can, to all the people you can, just as long as you can." Helping people and fellowshipping at her church gave her fulfillment and great joy.

So when you find yourself at a stage of life where you have accomplished everything you want to do professionally, setting new goals might mean setting some personal goals. If you like to travel, maybe you will make it your mission to visit all 50 states. If family brings you joy, you could make it your mission to mentor the young people in your family. Or you could be like my Aunt Dimple and just take joy in the happiness of other people and decide to "Do all the good you can, to all the people you can, just as long as you can!"

> "Do all the good you can, to all the people you can, just as long as you can!"
> Dimple Davis

Honestly, if you get to be like Aunt Dimple and continuously know what your next mission in life is going to be, it is a great feeling. When you never have to ask "What's next?" and you can just move from one mission, goal, or dream to the next one seamlessly, accomplishing your goals is a completely joyous experience. And that is the way I had been after accomplishing every major milestone before August 2016.

When I graduated this last time, I had to ask myself for the first time in over 18 years, "What's next?" That question can be a simple but daunting conundrum. Using myself as an example, I spent almost two decades pursuing a single dream. Every significant stride and accomplishment I have made in my life has been a progression towards that dream. Up until this point in my life, there had never been a time when I didn't know what the next step was. Truthfully, there were very few times in the past 20 years when I didn't know exactly what I would be doing in three to six months. There was always a new class, new extracurricular activity, new internship, or new school just over the horizon. With the exception of choosing between universities or job offers, I never had to question what was next.

What was even more reassuring about that lifestyle was that I never really had to question my ability to succeed. After 11 years of college and almost 23 years of school in general, I no longer had to question my ability to succeed in school. Sure, there were tests I wasn't confident about or subjects I struggled with, but on the whole, I knew how to prepare for a final exam, take a test, and/or write a paper. Thus, the experience of being in school was comfortable and known.

Furthermore, to be very honest, I had grown accustomed to being praised. After 20+ years of school, I knew how to do praiseworthy things in the classroom. To a great extent, though I acquired a lot of work and extracurricular experience along the way, my most praised and praiseworthy accomplishments were in the classroom. So not only was I leaving the comfort of the known, but I also risked losing that constant praise and reassurance.

I share this to underscore the anxiety and fear of moving into the next phase of life. Regardless of what I chose to do next, the phase of my life with final exams, graduations, and graduation parties was going to be over. On August 17th, when all the celebrations had ended and the graduation balloons had deflated and fallen to the ground, I was left with the question of "What's next?"

Note that after every graduation and every milestone in my life, I had been asked that question: "Now that you have done X, what's next?" In one form or another, I had heard that question for over a decade from other people. Yet what was uncomfortable, shocking, anxiety-causing, and flat-out terrifying was that after over a decade of being asked that question, for the first time, I said, "I don't know..." Thus, that became the first time I ever had to ask *myself* "What is next?"

> "I know from experience that you should never give up on yourself or others, no matter what."
> George Foreman

For some of you reading this, you may have reacted to those last paragraphs with bewilderment. You may be saying, "How could you be terrified after positioning yourself to do whatever you want?" That is a good thing. It likely means that, like my Aunt Dimple, you have generally progressed from one challenge to the next without much interruption. It is my sincere hope that whenever you accomplish your goals, your reaction is excitement, celebration, and an immediate resolve to progress to the next challenge.

However, if you find yourself having dedicated a significant portion of your life to a goal or a dream you are no longer pursuing and you feel haunted by the uncertainty you now face, this chapter was written specifically for you. The wording of the previous sentence is intentional—you may not have come to this uncertain "What's next?" phase because you have accomplished everything you wanted to achieve in the previous phase of life. And that is okay! This chapter is still for you.

I cannot unequivocally tell you how to get past this uncomfortable stage of your journey. Still, I can tell you what worked for me. In the months following my last graduation, I did five things: 1) *Remind*, 2) *Realize*, 3) *Recharge*, 4) *Re-engage*, and 5) *Repeat*.

5 R's of Restarting

REMIND

REALIZE

RECHARGE

RE-ENGAGE

REPEAT

First and foremost, the easiest thing to do when you are standing at the precipice of a new journey is to get discouraged. You start questioning whether you can succeed in this new phase of life. You can easily get down on yourself and really start to let fear and anxiety take ahold of you. In those moments, you want to "Remind."

Remind yourself of where you started from and how far you have come! Have you ever noticed that fitness programs always make you take pictures of yourself when you start? My reaction had always been to think: *What's the point of this? I am not going to show this to anyone else, and I am not going to forget what I look like.* But then I realized that was actually false. While in law school, I had gotten a bit more than a little chubby, and then started slimming down after I graduated and came back to Texas. Recently, I looked at an old picture of myself and was astonished that I looked so different.

Contrary to my belief, it is very easy to forget who you used to be. Growth is such a gradual process that you can easily ignore it when it is happening. In your mind, you are only comparing yourself to the way you were yesterday or an hour ago, and on that short time horizon, not much change occurs. But after months and years of progressing towards a goal, you will become a completely new person! Make a conscious effort to see that comparison and remind yourself how far you have come.

> "The future rewards those who press on. I don't have time to feel sorry for myself. I don't have time to complain. I'm going to press on."
> Pres. Barack Obama

Think about every milestone you have passed. Think about every interim goal you have achieved. Look at some old pictures of yourself and look at some of the old writing and work you produced. The more of that you do, the more you will internalize how much you have done.

At some point, let that reminder grow into a realization. Realize that the person who was able to accomplish all of those achievements has more they can do! Let that realization sink in and tell yourself, "I am just getting started!"

Once you "Remind" yourself of who you were and "Realize" how exceptional your transformation has been, it is time to "Recharge." In my experience, the best way to do this is to have some fun! I don't care how you feel, you need to celebrate! Revisit the chapter on celebrating your victories and celebrate the hard work you've done. Even if the last chapter of your life didn't end the way you wanted it to, you need to do something legitimately fun to celebrate that last phase closing. At the point when you have reminded yourself of how far you have come, you should have plenty to celebrate. Even if you feel like you don't have anything to celebrate, celebrate the fact that you are alive today! There are hundreds of thousands of people who didn't make it through yesterday. Another day is another opportunity. That alone is something to be celebrated!

It is important for you to celebrate, because you have worked hard and inherently accumulated stress you are probably unaware of—likely in the form of both mental and physical stress. If you have been pursuing your goals relentlessly, your body and mind might be locked in a perpetual state of tension, always ready to go to work.

This tension and the resulting readiness can be useful when you have a clear objective to pursue. However, it can also stifle your ability to think. The fun you have will give you a chance to relax that tension and make you better able to think about what the next phase of your life will look like.

"Celebration" doesn't just mean party—in fact, for most people, parties are not actually recharging/relaxing and instead become an additional source of stress. After my last graduation, yes, I had celebration parties, but that was not how I celebrated the milestone. Parties stress me out, plus they feel like a waste of money to me. Thus, to an extent, parties increase my tension rather than relieving it.

My actual celebration was traveling and visiting friends and family. I literally flew from coast to coast and took road trips all around Texas. In fact, I cranked out a large portion of this book as I was sitting seaside while visiting my friend in Bermuda, and I finished the first draft of it while attending a wedding in Las Vegas.

Make sure your celebration is what you enjoy doing and not what you feel like you have to do. Whenever you say "celebrate," don't automatically think of a party or travel. There are so many interesting activities and such a variety of people out there that everybody's

> "My vocation is my vacation. I love what I do."
> Nick Cannon

celebration can't possibly look the same. Whether it is going fishing, checking an item off of your bucket list, going to your favorite sporting events, doing the NASCAR racing experience, or golfing, do what makes you happy and do it to the fullest!

I spent the majority of my trip to Bermuda doing two-a-day workouts with my friend who is a former national heptathlete. That was fun for me, but as far as most people are concerned, that would be a horrible way to enjoy an island paradise. You are "supposed to" sunbathe, hang out at beaches, go to parties, and drink the night away. None of those things sound fun or relaxing to me. However, working out, ending the day with Netflix marathons, and writing was exceptionally relaxing for me.

There is no right or wrong answer for how you should celebrate as long as you do *something* and you don't hurt yourself or others. I do not recommend sitting around your house staring at the ceiling. If you don't want to leave the house, do an indoor activity. Read some books, workout, build some things, play some games you thoroughly enjoy, or basically do anything that will keep you from being idle with your thoughts. There is nothing more annoying than being inactive or stuck with your thoughts when you are in the midst of uncertainty. Your mind will not relax unless you force it to focus on something relaxing.

Next, you must "Re-engage" and pursue a goal. I do not mean another dream or major milestone goal. At this point, just find something to do that challenges you.

This may unfold naturally as you are celebrating. While you are trying to celebrate, you may find yourself drawn to certain activities, and those activities may turn into interim goals. Examples of this could be getting in better shape for the people who celebrate by working out, repairing your house for the people who like do-it-yourself projects, or even writing a book for people like me who like to write.

Additionally, based on your previous experiences, you may have people approach you with projects to work on. Examples of this could be leaders of organizations you are affiliated with asking you for help or even former or current colleagues requesting your assistance with work-related projects. Get involved with these opportunities.

Ultimately, it is your responsibility to find something to re-engage with. If this does not occur naturally during or at the termination of your celebration, find something to do. If you can't think of anything, consider working on a cause that resonates with you. Remember, this does not need to be a major milestone, just something you can work towards and feel accomplished once you have completed it.

> "Sometimes it's the journey that teaches you a lot about the destination."
> Aubrey Drake Graham

The reason doing so is important is that it helps to keep you out of a rut—when you are *not* pursuing a goal, it is easy to fall into a rut. What do I mean by "a rut"? It is a cycle of negative feelings towards yourself that can cause you to be unproductive, and it is a cycle that is hard to change. The way it tends to work is that you start feeling like you are wasting your days away, so you get down on yourself. Being down on yourself causes you to have less energy and do less with your days. As a result, you feel worse about wasting more time... And the cycle continues.

Break this cycle and/or prevent it from starting by picking a goal to pursue in the interim.

Additionally, although it shouldn't matter what other people think, most of us are not completely immune to caring. As such, it may bother us to be asked "What are you up to?" when the answer is "Nothing." Re-engaging gives you something to talk about in such conversations, which in turn makes you less likely to fall into a rut.

The final step is to return to the first chapter of this book and "Repeat" the process of establishing and aggressively pursuing new dreams. There is no need to reinvent the wheel! You can go through the same process you used to figure out and pursue your last dream to create a new one.

I will add one more piece of advice. During the re-engaging process, did you find yourself invariably drawn to a particular activity that you thoroughly enjoyed? If so, consider this: *that activity might make the basis for a new dream*! There are people who make careers out of doing everything from buying clothes to traveling the world. Whatever your passion is, there is a way to succeed doing it.

Going forward, the important thing to realize is that every ending is a new beginning. Whenever you close one chapter of your life, you are automatically opening a new chapter. Don't ever let yourself get caught up in your past mistakes or past triumphs. Doing so can make you miss the exceptional moments of the present and leave you unprepared to face the future.

> "During your life, never stop dreaming.
> No one can take away your dreams."
> Tupac Shakur

Chapter 16:
My Secret to Success!

Whenever I speak in front of an audience of students, I begin by saying, "If you are attentive until the end, I will give you my secret to raising your GPA without additional studying," adding the caveat, "You still will have to study for this to work."

Then at the end of the presentation, I display a picture of my mom hooding me at my PhD graduation next to the quote, "Your attitude determines your altitude [in life]." My mom used this phrase all of the time. It was her way of saying that regardless of how intelligent or talented I was, the single greatest determinate of my success in life would be my attitude and how I treated others—internalizing that lesson is my secret to academic, professional and personal success!

Whether you are a student trying to get a GPA bump, a young professional trying to build your team of coaches and mentors, a seasoned professional trying to attract the attention of a sponsor for career advancement, or an entrepreneur fundraising and securing cofounders, at some point in your life you will need someone to show you favor—even when you haven't earned it. This type of favoritism can be something as simple as granting you an extension on a project or something as big as investing a million dollars in your business. In the moments when you need someone to take an irrational interest in your success, it will be your attitude that decides your success.

Ultimately, once you get beyond the Scantron & purely multiple-choice tests of primary school, your performance is evaluated subjectively. Even in your objective subject matter (e.g., math, science, etc.), you are still graded subjectively because of partial credit. As such, your success will oftentimes be determined by your professor's perception of you and your understanding. If they perceive you to be an A student, they will view your mistakes as anomalous and find ways to give you more partial credit; whereas, if they perceive you to be a C or D student, your grade will change accordingly.

Similarly, when you encounter the tests of life, your evaluations are subjective. On your job, you are reviewed on both your outcomes and your supervisor's perception of you. Most studies show that people who take time to engage in effective networking (i.e., positively impacting how they are perceived) receive more favorable evaluations and are promoted faster than people who solely focus on work product. If you are seen as a great employee/leader, people will treat you—and reward you—as such.

Even in the world of entrepreneurship, your reputation and people's perception of you makes all the difference. Everyone has good ideas; when someone invests in your business, they are investing in you and not your ideas. If people believe you will be successful, they will invest in you—whereas, if they don't believe in you, they won't invest in your business! Thus, successful entrepreneurs are people with an attitude that rallies others to their cause.

What type of attitude makes people want to grant you "irrational favor" in your academic, professional and business pursuits? My brother Ray answered this question best: "*You have to be likable!*" Likable is not the same thing as being liked—being "likable" is something that you do, whereas being "liked" is other people's perception. As previously stated, you cannot control how people are going to perceive you. You can only control how you act and how you treat other people.

So how can you have a good likable attitude? For me, I broke these pieces of advice into three simple rules: *Be Respectful*, *Be Passionate*, and *Be Thankful*. Though a simple creed, this has been the secret to all of my success.

- BE RESPECTFUL -

"We all require and want respect, man or woman, black or white. It's our basic human right."
Aretha Franklin

Treat everyone you meet with respect and dignity. And when I say everyone, I mean *everyone*. People tend to find this the most difficult when they are dealing with someone they deem to be "unimportant" or someone who has wronged them.

It is a grave mistake to pass judgment on the importance of people. You never know the impact they may have on your life. For example, I cannot tell you how many times I have seen people disrespect custodians and administrative assistants. This is a huge mistake! You would be surprised at the amount of face time that the people you may write off as "unimportant" get with the "important" people. When your boss' boss is burning the midnight oil, oftentimes the custodians are the only other people in the building. You would be surprised how many CEOs and presidents know the person who cleans their office on a first-name basis. There have even been highly successful people who used custodians as a means to gather information about the personality, character, and intentions of people they were vetting for a business relationship, hiring, or promotion.

Also, I learned early on that most successful people don't actually control their own schedules. The VPs, CEOs, presidents, icons, world-renowned personalities, etc. you are trying to get as mentors and sponsors go where their administrators tell them to go. Thus, the administrative assistant whom you may ignore is often the ultimate gatekeeper to getting those life-changing meetings. I cannot tell you the number of times I have gotten on a person's calendar at the last minute (sometimes even bumping another person from their time slot) because I treated the administrators, assistants, and secretaries with the same respect with which I treated the "people in charge."

A large part of the reason I was able to graduate when I did and successfully accomplish my academic dreams was because of Yvonne Burrell, the Administrative Associate for the School of Engineering. In June of 2016, I told Mrs. Yvonne that in order to graduate, I needed a signed approval from the Associate Dean of the School of Engineering in fewer than 48 hours. Fortunately, every time I had seen her for the past three years, I had shown her the respect she was due, so when I came to her asking her to do something in two days that normally took two weeks, she had my back—Mrs. Yvonne personally walked my authorizations to the Associate Dean's office, interrupted a meeting, and got me the signature I needed. In fewer than three minutes, she returned, handed me the signed authorization, and congratulated me on graduating. Because of her, I graduated two months later. Respect is something that is free to give and invaluable when returned.

"I'm not concerned with your liking or disliking me... All I ask is that you respect me as a human being."
Jackie Robinson

Similarly, disrespecting people who wrong you is a pointless exercise that can have a negative impact on your success. Another southern idiom is "Two wrongs don't make a right." Behaving disrespectfully is wrong, even when it is done to somebody who has harmed you. People are constantly watching and evaluating you. If a potential mentor or sponsor sees you disrespecting someone, it will not matter what the other person did—they will only see what you are doing and will likely develop a negative opinion of your personality. So I ask, "Is expressing your disdain for a person you dislike worth sabotaging yourself?"

Additionally, by allowing somebody to alter your temperament, you have given them control over you. When you feel like your blood is boiling and you feel your pulse strengthening with rage at the sight of someone, that person's presence is sending your body into a panic. What you are feeling is your body straining your heart, expending your energy, increasing your blood pressure, and quickening your pulse. The feeling of warmth is the capillaries being stretched with the added pressure and blood flow. And all of this is putting you at a greater risk of heart attack, stroke, and death. Do you value your hatred of that person more than you value your life? And don't you think it is problematic that you are giving somebody you don't like dominion over your mind and so much control over your body?

You do not have to befriend people who harm you, but being able to show everyone a base level of respect is essential. By finding a way to show respect, you force yourself to let go of your animosity (which improves your health). When you can let go of the past, it is a truly freeing experience. This is beneficial because then the mental capacity that is no longer allocated to thinking of snide remarks or ways to "one-up them" can be applied to more aggressively pursuing your goals. Remember, you do not respect people for *their* benefit, you respect them for *yours*.

> "It's not an easy journey, to get to a place where you forgive people. But it is such a powerful place, because it frees you."
> Tyler Perry

- BE PASSIONATE -

This entire book has been about making your dreams come true. When you choose a dream to pursue, make it a dream you can be passionate about! Life is too short to pursue things that do not stir your soul.

Because my dad died when I was ten years old, I don't have many memories of him. What I do remember was how passionate he was about fixing things. This applied to everything from cars and tractors to people and lives. Whether it was opening our home to guests so that they could get back on their feet or getting under cars in his Sunday best after church to bring a dead car back to life, fixing things was his passion. He loved being able to take what others saw as trash and restore them to being treasures. He loved it so much that he did it whether it was his spare time or for work and whether it was for pay or for free. Seeing that, I understood that life is more complete when you are doing something that you can be that passionate about.

When you find something you can pursue with that kind of passion, pursue it!

- Be Thankful -

I know it is popular to talk about being "self-made." I am sure some people will look at my history and call me "self-made." I came from a single-parent household, grew up without much money, helped pay bills since I was ten years old, and moved out on my own a week after my 15th birthday. To go from that to being the youngest engineer in the nation, the youngest licensed attorney in the state of Texas, and having a PhD before the age of 26, I could probably be the very definition of "self-made." But ultimately, there is no such thing as a self-made person.

> "There is no limit to the amount of good you can do if you don't care who gets the credit."
>
> Pres. Ronald Reagan

Regardless of how much you've had to do on your own, it is impossible to succeed without the help of others. It could be a parent or sibling who sacrificed so that you could afford to pursue your dreams, a person who took a risk by giving you an opportunity, or someone who took time out of their day to give you some life-changing advice. If you struggle to think of someone who helped you, just remember that no baby has ever changed their own diapers. Whatever the case, we all have people in our lives who have helped us get to where we are and will help us get to where we want to be.

Sometimes, the people who make us who we are will be people we know intimately; other times, it will be people we have never met and never will. Think about the people who fight for your freedoms in the armed forces; the people who create the medical techniques, vaccines, and cures that keep you alive; the activists and community leaders who fight for your rights; the officers who protect you from threats you will never see…the list goes on.

There are so many people who work for you to have health, safety, security, and opportunity! With all of them in mind, how can any of us ever claim to be truly "self-made"?

When people spend time, money, effort, or influence to help you achieve, never forget to take the time to express your gratitude. In some cases, we have the opportunity to thank the people who most impact our daily lives. When those opportunities arise, I encourage you to tell people "Thank you!"

In other cases, you will not be able to properly thank those who have supported you. In those contexts, I believe we should all remember the adage "Imitation is the most sincere form of flattery." When people deposit into you, imitate their behavior and deposit into others. You will never regret the time you take out of your day to selflessly help others.

This book is my attempt at following my own advice—I wanted to deposit into others all that has been deposited into me as a thank-you to everyone who made me the man I am today. I cannot properly thank all of those people who have contributed to who I am, but I can express gratitude to you, the reader. Thank you for reading this book! I appreciate the time and effort it took to do so. Please apply the principles herein to make your dreams come true. And when the dreams you dream do come true, don't forget to help others do the same.

> "When the dreams you're dreamin' come to you,
> when the work you put in is realized,
> let yourself feel the pride, but
> **always stay humble and kind.**"
> Tim McGraw

Acknowledgments

First and foremost thanks be to God; without Him I could not have accomplished anything that I have done, which includes writing this book. Thank you again to everyone who helped make this book a reality. Thank you to everyone who has inspired me over the years, and continues to inspire me to this day. And thank you to my personal team and my support network; you all know who you are, and you made me who I am.

Even though that covers everyone, I would be remised if I didn't make some special acknowledgments.

Thank you to my editing team for the great work they did: Dr. Tanya Dugat Wickliff (aka Mom), Lisa Howard, Megan Hudson, Semaj Fields, Brittani 'Tani' Saeun, Whitley Brock, Raymond Wickliff, Jamar Dugat, and Haben Girma. Your input was invaluable to finishing this project. Also, thanks to the people over at Grammarly, Inc. for developing a solid proofreading program. It got me through my dissertation and two editions of this book, so I am supremely appreciative.

I want to thank the people at Rice University for all of their support. Thank you to Translee, Syd, and The Internet for making some great writing music; it definitely got me through the home stretch.

Thank you to the beautiful country of Bermuda and my Bermudian friends for being so welcoming. I especially want to thank Andrea Jackson-Hinds for opening her home to me and for not being bothered by my feverish typing at random hours of the day and night.

Las Vegas, NV will always have a special place in my heart because it was where I finished the first draft of the first edition of this book. Thank you to the Walton's for allowing me to be MIA for a lot of your pre-wedding festivities.

Thank you to my mentor and friend Tavis Smiley and the Smiley Books team for all the guidance. This process would have been incredibly difficult without your support.

Thank you to Chester D.T. Baldwin for encouraging me to focus on finishing this book. I appreciate the vote of confidence, and I have not forgotten that this is only item #1 on the to-do list you gave me.

I couldn't publish my first book without acknowledging my families' hometowns – Ames, Dayton, Liberty and Raywood (i.e. Liberty County); a special thanks to Judge Jay H. Knight and my cousin Robert-Anthony for honoring me as a native son of Liberty County. No matter where life takes me I will never forget where I come from!

And I could not forget to acknowledge the State of Texas that I love. Whether it was getting my first car in Round Rock, opening my college acceptance letter from the Texas Academy of Mathematics & Science in my living room in Pflugerville, attending my first college class at the Univ. of North Texas in Denton, starting my first job in Ames, driving to DFW for prom, becoming an engineer in Houston, becoming Dr. Wickliff in Aggieland (College Station) or finishing the second edition of this book in Missouri City, my personal journey has been inextricably linked to Texas. For that reason, I love every corner of my state from the canyons in the Pan Handle to the beaches in the south and from the deserts out in West Texas to Liberty County in the east. I hope to one day visit every place in between!

If you have read this far, I want to thank you for being so engaged. I hope you got something useful out of this book; use it to grow, and pass that knowledge along!

Sincerely

Cortlan J. W.

I want to hear from you! Follow me on social media to give and get updates. Also, take a picture of yourself with this book and share it on my social media pages.

 www.**YoungAndDriven**.com

 www.Instagram.com/**CJWickliff**

 www.Twitter.com/**CJWickliff**

 www.Facebook.com/**YoungAndDrivenBook**

For booking information:

www.CortlanWickliff.com

- or -

Cortlan.Wickliff@gmail.com

*If you are **Audacious** enough to dream, **Bold** enough to try, and **Courageous** enough to try again, then you will always be on the right track to making your dreams come true.*

Made in the
USA
Lexington, KY